Praise For
The Alcohol Experiment

'Day 60 alcohol free (AF). Just did karaoke sober. I didn't know that was possible. I had even given myself permission to have one cocktail (to loosen the vocal cords, you understand?). But after looking through the menu, I just didn't fancy anything! Stuck with water all night. Now on the train heading home, looking forward to waking up tomorrow with a clear head, money in my pocket, my dignity (if you ignore the singing), and possibly a sore throat. The Alcohol Experiment is incredible. Thank you.'   *M.K., London, England*

'Thank YOU for this amazing gift you have given so many with first your book and now the Alcohol Experiment! It has truly been life changing for me, and at three months alcohol-free tomorrow, I am more hopeful than I have been in a very long time.'

L.K., Windsor, England

'Day 60! What? Always dreamed of being AF. Didn't think it was possible. Thank you for my life, Annie Grace!'

O.F., Dublin, Ireland

'45 days alcohol free. I didn't think I could make it through the first week, and now I can't imagine ever drinking again. The Alcohol Experiment saved my life. It's so worth the journey!'

R.D., New York, New York

'Annie Grace, I just wanted you to know you've touched the lives of many people. This is such a huge movement that you started. I just want to thank you from the bottom of my heart (tears are coming down right now). You saved me after almost 27 years of drinking daily, since I was 13 years old when I started. I never thought I would be able to do what I am doing now. Thank you.'

S.J., Sydney, Australia

'Your 30-day experiment was so helpful. I learned so much! I'm well on my way to being AF completely – from drinking daily to drinking five times in 110 days. And I don't plan on drinking anytime soon. It was so in-depth and educational. Thank you.'

G.P., Austin, Texas

'31 days ago, I started your alcohol-free experiment. I haven't touched any alcohol in the past month and cannot thank you enough for giving me the kick in the a** to get started! Thank you, thank you, thank you.'

C.R., Costa Mesa, California

'You are changing the lives of so many people. Thank you. I feel like someone woke me up from a very, very long nightmare. Really, Groundhog Day. There are no words to express my gratitude. Thank you, Annie Grace, for saving my life.'

B.K.R., Portland, Maine

'I've been wanting to message you for a while to say thank you. I've been trying to moderate my drinking for years and find it's a daily fight. Having a dad and brother who are alcoholics, I was resigned to the fact it runs in the family! My sister introduced me to the Alcohol Experiment after I had just completed Dry January – wow! It absolutely changed my perspective on alcohol, and I haven't touched a drop since, nor do I intend to! Thank you so much for setting me free.'

I.G., Brisbane, Australia

'I am now 37 days AF and have never felt so relaxed and happy. I just want to thank you for caring enough to create the Alcohol Experiment. Without your support I wouldn't be where I am. I wouldn't be going to a weekend of camping and family fun looking forward to not drinking. It's made such a difference to my life. You make me feel humble and so, so grateful. Thank you.'

F. C., Brooklyn, New York

'Thank you so, so much, Annie. You are such an amazing force for good in this world! The Alcohol Experiment changed my life.'

H.R.T., Palm Beach, Florida

THE ALCOHOL EXPERIMENT

30 DAYS TO TAKE CONTROL, CUT DOWN OR GIVE UP FOR GOOD

ANNIE GRACE

ONE PLACE. MANY STORIES

HQ
An imprint of HarperCollins*Publishers* Ltd
1 London Bridge Street
London SE1 9GF

This paperback edition 2018

8

First published in Great Britain by
HQ, an imprint of HarperCollins*Publishers* Ltd 2018

A catalogue record for this book is
available from the British Library.

ISBN: 978-0-00-829347-5

Printed and bound in Great Britain by
CPI Group (UK) Ltd, Croydon CR0 4YY

MIX
Paper from
responsible sources
FSC™ C007454

Turner, Trace, and Daelyn.
You are why I dream of a better tomorrow.

Brian. My favorite person.
Thank you for creating this life with me.
Thank you for trusting me enough to double down
on this dream and follow the road wherever it leads.

Jesus. Your Grace. Your Love. Your Mercy.
Your Breath in my lungs.

Contents

Introduction 1

DAY 1:   *What's Your Why?* 19

ACT #1:   The Taste of Alcohol 22

DAY 2:   *It's Not What You Give Up, But What You GAIN* 28

DAY 3:   *Why We Think We Like to Drink* 34

ACT #2:   Alcohol and Sleep 38

DAY 4:   *Dealing with Discomfort* 42

DAY 5:   *What Are Cravings, Really?* 47

DAY 6:   *Why Willpower Doesn't Work for Long* 52

ACT #3:   Alcohol, Relaxation, and Stress Relief 56

DAY 7:   *Your Experiment and Your Friends* 61

DAY 8:   *How Alcohol Affects Your Senses* 66

DAY 9:   *The Power of Self-Talk* 70

ACT #4:   Alcohol, Our Culture, and Society _____ 79

DAY 10:   *Dealing with Sugar Cravings* _____ 86

DAY 11:   *The Alcohol Culture Is Shifting* _____ 92

ACT #5:   Alcohol and Happiness _____ 96

DAY 12:   *Your Incredible Body and Brain* _____ 103

ACT #6:   Is Alcohol Healthy in Moderation? _____ 107

DAY 13:   *Let's Talk About Sex* _____ 113

DAY 14:   *Staying Mindful in the Midst of Chaos* _____ 118

ACT #7:   Alcohol and Parenting (a.k.a. Mommy Juice) _____ 122

DAY 15:   *Social Life and Dating* _____ 130

DAY 16:   *The Power of Belief* _____ 135

ACT #8:   Alcohol Is My Friend _____ 140

DAY 17:   *Relieving Boredom Without Drinking* _____ 145

DAY 18:   *Why Tolerance Is Literally a Buzzkill* _____ 151

DAY 19:   *Dealing with Depression* _____ 156

DAY 20:   *Our Headline Culture and the Science of Sharing* _____ 160

DAY 21:   *Hey, Good Lookin'!* _____ 165

DAY 22:   *Drinking Due to Unmet Needs* _____ 170

ACT #9: Alcohol and Sadness _____ **174**

DAY 23: *Alcohol's Effect on Your Health* _____ **179**

ACT #10: Alcohol and Anger _____ **186**

DAY 24: *Are Addictive Personalities Real?* _____ **191**

DAY 25: *Setbacks and the Way Forward* _____ **194**

DAY 26: *Liberation vs. Fixation* _____ **198**

DAY 27: *Is Alcohol Really Poisonous and Addictive?* _____ **201**

DAY 28: *The Truth About Moderation* _____ **208**

DAY 29: *Tough Love* _____ **213**

DAY 30: *What's Next?* _____ **219**

One Final Word _____ **229**

Acknowledgments _____ **233**

Appendix _____ **235**

Notes _____ **237**

Introduction

It's YOUR body . . .

It's YOUR mind . . .

It's YOUR choice . . .

During the Alcohol Experiment, you'll make a choice to go 30 days without alcohol. Just to see how you feel. You'll become a detached reporter, researching the facts, writing down your observations, and possibly drawing new conclusions. This is an exciting experiment, not a punishment. You're not weak-willed for questioning your drinking. There's no judgment or labeling here. You have a unique opportunity to remember how to enjoy life without alcohol. And with this book's unconventional approach, I'm willing to bet you'll enjoy the process!

▍WHO IS THIS FOR?

This experiment is for you if you're curious about your relationship with alcohol, and you're thinking about drinking less often or not at all.

It is also for you if

- You are of two minds about alcohol—you want to drink less but you also feel deprived or upset when you abstain.
- You drink out of habit or boredom—only to regret it later.

- You are starting to wonder if alcohol is taking more than it is giving.
- You are curious about a life without booze but do not feel you are an alcoholic.
- You want to drink less, but life is just too stressful.
- You have a love-hate relationship with alcohol—and find yourself setting limits and then breaking them when happy hour rolls around.
- You have tried to cut back or stop drinking (possibly many times) using willpower alone and found it ineffective.
- You fell into drinking more than you ever wanted—without making a conscious decision to do so.
- You can stop drinking for a few days but find yourself feeling deprived.
- You are ready to regain control—of your drinking, your life, your health, and your happiness.
- You are looking forward to feeling great on Saturday night *and* Sunday morning.
- You are ready to be your best self, get in shape, regain your self-esteem, and change your life.

It's NOT for you if you have a strong physical addiction to alcohol—if you are physically dependent and suffer from serious withdrawal symptoms, such as delirium tremens or hallucinations, when you attempt to stop or cut back. This book may help with your emotional and psychological addiction by changing your perspective and erasing your desire to drink. However, I am not a doctor, and alcohol withdrawal can be extremely dangerous. You should seek professional medical assistance so your detoxification is medically supervised.

Is life better without alcohol? That's up to you to decide. My own experience with this experiment proved that, for me, life was absolutely better when I chose not to drink. However, your experience might be different. It's your body. It's your mind. It's your choice. I'm simply inviting you to open your mind to the possibility of making a different choice and then encouraging you to see how it changes things in your daily life.

It's 30 days, not forever . . . Many people ask me if they will have to give up drinking forever if they try the experiment. My answer is it's up to them. My only goal is to offer you a shift in your perspective and to show you some of the neuroscience behind why you might be drinking more than you'd like to.

You might go back to your regular drinking habits after the 30 days, you might drink a bit more mindfully (and less often), or you might decide to give it another 30 days just for the heck of it. You might also decide you feel so good you never want to go back.

Whatever you decide, I'd love to hear your experience with the experiment. If you'd like to share your story, email me at hello@alcoholexperiment.com.

WHY WE DRINK MORE THAN WE WANT TO

Since you're reading this right now, you're probably questioning how much you drink. Maybe you know you drink too much and want to quit. Or maybe you're just curious about what life is like with a bit less alcohol. Maybe you're questioning whether you might be overdoing it a bit. No matter where you are on the spectrum, you're not alone. I've been there. And tens of thousands of people inside the Alcohol Experiment community have been there, too. You're probably wondering why in the world you keep drinking even though you've made a conscious decision to cut back or stop altogether. Why do we do things we no longer want to do?

I wondered the same thing. When I first started drinking, it seemed to be a natural, normal thing to do. I saw nothing wrong with it. I didn't know all the negative ways alcohol could affect my health. I was a drinker, and I was proud of it. I tried hard to develop a tolerance so I could keep up with my colleagues. It was fun. It was relaxing. I had better sex when I was drunk.

. . . Or so I thought.

Eventually, I came to a point in my life when I started to question my drinking. I didn't like waking up with a hangover. I didn't like having to piece together conversations and wondering if I said or did anything embarrassing. I wasn't even enjoying myself anymore. I could drink two bottles of wine and not even feel it because I had such a high tolerance. So I made a conscious decision to stop drinking. And I thought that would be it. I just wouldn't drink. Easy-peasy.

Sound familiar?

If you've tried to give up or moderate your alcohol consumption in the past and failed, I want you to know it's not your fault. There's something going on you're probably not aware of. And once you understand it, your eyes will be opened and you'll be able to undergo this experiment in a meaningful way. It won't be just another failure of willpower.

To understand what's going on, we need to explore a concept called cognitive dissonance. *Cognitive* means "the way you think." And *dissonance* means "disagreement." So, cognitive dissonance is when there's a disagreement in your thinking. Well, how can that be? You've got one brain, right? Actually, your brain has many parts, and they can come into conflict with one another. But what we're really talking about here is your conscious mind and your subconscious mind. Your conscious mind is everything you're aware of. You're tired of waking up with a headache. You don't like spending your money on alcohol. Maybe your relationship is suffering, or your kids don't even know you anymore. Because you're aware of those things, you make a conscious decision to stop drinking.

Ahh, but there's another powerful part of your mind: your subconscious. That's where you've stored a lifetime of subconscious conditioning and beliefs that, by definition, you're unaware of. Our subconscious mind controls our emotions and desires. And society's attitudes about alcohol are programmed and fixed in our subconscious minds by the media, our parents, our friends, and our role models. We don't consciously adopt these beliefs. They are imprinted on us. Take, for example, the belief that drinking helps you relax. That's a belief you formed a long time ago after careful observation and experience. You weren't born with this knowledge. But you watched your parents drink after a long day. You've seen movies and TV shows where characters drink to relax. And you've experienced it yourself and found it to be true. So you formed a strong belief that alcohol helps you relax.

Here's the thing about subconscious beliefs—they're not always true. We form our belief systems when we're very young, and sometimes we'll carry those beliefs our whole lives without ever questioning them. Most of the time, this is fine. The sky is blue. Ice is cold. If I fall down, it's going to hurt. Cognitive dissonance happens when one of our subconscious beliefs disagrees with a conscious desire or decision. If I believe alcohol helps me relax, but I've decided not to drink after work anymore, that's a problem! Part of me desperately wants a drink to unwind after a long day, and another part of me doesn't want to overdo it and wake up with a hangover. There are two conflicting desires. Cognitive dissonance. To drink or not to drink, that is the question.

This is one of the reasons we continue to drink more than we want to even after we've decided to cut back. This is why willpower doesn't work in the long term. *Merriam-Webster*'s dictionary defines *willpower* as "energetic determination." That means it takes energy, conscious thought, and effort. This is especially true when you are trying to stop doing something that you believe provides a benefit. We don't have to exert conscious effort and energy not to drink something we believe is bad for us if we see no benefit in it. For example, there is no effort involved in turning down a glass of motor oil.

If you believe, even subconsciously, that alcohol provides a benefit, you will be exercising willpower to cut back or avoid drinking. The problem with willpower is that since it is energy, willpower runs out. And if you use your willpower on one thing—like being patient with your kids or paying attention during a boring work event—you will have less willpower to use when you try to turn down that next drink.

That is why I say we need to get out of the willpower game altogether. Until we resolve the inner conflict, we cannot hope to succeed.

Let's pretend we're trying to avoid sweets because we're trying to lose weight. Yet someone at the office brings in a big plate of freshly baked cookies and we mindlessly grab one and eat it. (Okay, who are we kidding . . . we eat like three cookies.) Bam! Dissonance. Your brain doesn't want to eat cookies, because you're on a diet. But you did. There's an internal conflict. Our brains immediately try to restore internal harmony in a few ways:

1. We can change our behavior. Make a vow not to eat another cookie no matter how good they look.

2. We can justify our behavior and say, "Oh, it's okay to cheat every once in a while. We all need a little sugar now and then. I deserve it."

3. We can add another behavior to counteract the first one. "Well, I ate the cookies, but that's okay. I'll go for a long run after work to burn off the extra calories."

4. We can delude ourselves by denying or ignoring the conflicting information. "Those cookies are probably not all that bad for my diet. They seemed pretty small anyway."

We delude ourselves all the time when it comes to alcohol or any addictive substance. We ignore the fact that alcohol isn't doing us any favors and it's actually harming us. We do it as a defense mechanism because we're trying to solve this internal disagreement. Conflict hurts. Humans are hardwired to avoid it whenever possible. When you're divided—when you're not whole—it's incredibly painful. And what do we drinkers do to numb pain? We drink! And then we drink more. And sometimes we drink until we black out to avoid something painful, even temporarily.

The more we drink, the worse we feel (mentally and physically) and the more we don't want to drink.

The more we don't want to drink, the more internal conflict we create.

The more conflict, the more pain.

The more pain, the more we drink.

It's a cycle that spirals out of control. It's not intentional. We may not even know we're doing it until something terrible happens. At some point, we wake up to the reality and try to change. But unless we address the dissonance, change continually eludes us. I tried to drink less, to set limits on my drinking. I could do it for a little while, but eventually my willpower would give out, and I'd be right back to waking up wondering how many glasses I'd had the night before. I felt helpless. I felt weak. And I felt alone. I'm smart and capable. Why did this have such a hold on me? I would intend to drink a single glass of wine, or maybe two, but would wake up the next morning being unable to count how many I'd had. And that would make me want to drink more because then I wouldn't have to think about the fact that I'd broken a commitment to myself—again. Drinking erased the conflict, even for a little while.

What I didn't know was that there was something much bigger at work. The subconscious mind is where our desires originate. So part of me was so much stronger than my conscious desire to get my act together. The deck was stacked against me, and I didn't even realize it.

The good news is that I discovered a way to truly resolve my cognitive dissonance around drinking. And it works for anything, by the way. If you're eating sugar when you don't want to, or you're gambling when you don't want to, or you're watching too much television—whatever. This method works to resolve the conflict and get your conscious and subconscious minds on the same page. When that happens, you get what you want with no effort. You can go to a party with all your friends and have a great time without even thinking about alcohol. You can ring in the New Year with ginger ale. You can save your relationships. You can change your life.

Want to know the secret?

It's all about awareness. If you're struggling because you're unaware of your subconscious beliefs, then the solution is to become aware of them. Shine a light deep into the nooks and crannies of your mind and figure out what beliefs are holding you back. What beliefs are in conflict with your desire to drink less or stop drinking?

I've developed a proven, scientifically based process to do exactly that. The process is based on a technique called Liminal Thinking, created by the bestselling author Dave Gray, and The Work, by author Byron Katie. The liminal space is the area between your conscious and your subconscious, or subliminal, mind. The technique I've developed is called ACT: Awareness, Clarity, and Turnaround. You're going to become aware of your belief by naming and putting language to it. Next, you clarify the belief, where it came from and how it feels inside you. Finally, you will turn around the belief coming up with a few reasons why the opposite of your long-held belief may be truer or as true as the original belief. As with many of the most profound tools for change, it is a simple process of deconstructing your beliefs by asking yourself questions like these:

What do I believe?

Is it true?

How does it make me feel?

Is it helpful?

Remember when I said sometimes our beliefs just aren't true? Well, that's how you untangle this mess—by discovering the truth. Does alcohol truly relax you? Or do you just think it does? Do you really enjoy sex more when you're drunk? Or does it become a sloppy, embarrassing mess you can barely remember?

I'm not going to suggest the answer is one or the other. I can't make you believe something you don't want to believe. Your subconscious beliefs remain deeply entrenched until *you* become aware of them and decide to change them by questioning their validity. Every few days during this 30-day experiment, you'll see bonus ACT chapters. You can read them as they come up, or you can read them first if you like. These special chapters present you with some facts regarding certain common beliefs about alcohol. All I ask is for you to keep an open mind and carefully consider what you're reading. It might take a few days or weeks of mulling it over before you decide one way or another. You might need to test out some theories. That's okay. Take as much time as you need. This is your experiment. Here's a preview of how the ACT technique works:

▍ THE ACT TECHNIQUE

1. **AWARENESS.** Name your belief. In the context of alcohol, this is your conscious reason for drinking, simply put it into words:

   Alcohol relaxes me.

2. **CLARITY.** Discover *why* you believe it and *where* it originated. You do this by asking questions—both of yourself and of the external evidence—and uncovering truths about your belief.

   What have I observed that supports this belief?

   Happy hour. And the idea that everyone unwinds with a cocktail after a stressful day at work.

   Every time I talk to my friends about my struggles, either with my kids or husband, they always say something like, "Oh, no! Don't worry, I know just the thing—you need some wine immediately!"

   What are my experiences with alcohol and relaxation?

I've felt the relaxing effects of alcohol myself. After a stressful day at work, a drink seems to calm my nerves and allows me to transition from the hard workday to a relaxing evening.

Then it's time to do some detective work and compare this belief with both your internal and external realities. Internally, you will ask yourself questions like these:

What do I mean by "relax"?

How do I feel when I'm not relaxed?

How do I feel when I am relaxed?

Does anything else make me feel the same way?

How do I feel while I'm drinking? Is that the same feeling as "relaxed"?

How do I feel the next day? Is that relaxed?

Is it true, scientifically? Does alcohol relax human beings?

Externally, you will examine the evidence. Does research support this belief? What do external sources say about this belief? Do they support or contradict it? And don't worry, you won't have to do a bunch of research—throughout the 30 days of the experiment I'll be supplying the studies and data.

3. **TURNAROUND.** This is where you allow your subconscious to let go of the belief, deciding if after exploration it is indeed true for you. There are two steps here.

First, you turn the initial belief around and find as many ways as you can that the opposite of your initial belief is true. For example, if your belief is *"alcohol relaxes me"* the opposite becomes *"alcohol does not relax me"* or *"alcohol stresses me out."*

Now that you've stated the opposite, come up with as many reasons as you can that the opposite is as true as or truer than the original belief. Examples might include

- Alcohol stresses my body out; a hangover is evidence of that.

- Alcohol prevents me from taking the action necessary to truly relieve my stress, so in that case it does not relax me.

- When I drink, I am more likely to get in an argument with my spouse, and fighting is stressful.

- When I drink, I beat myself up about it the next day, and that is stressful.

Once you've done that, the final step is simply to decide if this belief still holds true for you and if it is serving you or if you would be better off letting it go.

ACT: Awareness. Clarity. Turnaround. It's an effective, scientific way to shine a light into your subconscious and figure out what's actually causing your behavior. And you can find a guided worksheet in the back of this book to apply this process to any belief that comes up about alcohol, or about anything else in your life.

The important thing to remember is that there is no wrong answer! You are not messing up if you go through this process and still feel the belief is true for you. I know it sounds counterintuitive, but trust me on this—this process is about presenting your subconscious mind with information, facts, and logic. It's about shifting your mind-set. And while that can often happen quickly by simply reading through the ACT chapters, it can also happen more slowly over time. Again, there are no wrong answers.

Now you know there's something deeper at work here, and there's something you can do about it, I hope you're excited about this experiment! My ACT technique works. You can use it to enact change in so many areas of your life. It's so empowering. You can use it to lose weight, start exercising, stop procrastinating, and be a better parent. For now, though, let's focus on your drinking.

STICKING WITH IT

Often we don't think about how much we drink or why we drink—like we're doing in this experiment—until drinking is no longer an option. We don't know if we drink because there's chaos in our lives, or if there's chaos because we drink. Suddenly, when the option to escape through drinking isn't there, we're forced to take a look at what's going on in our lives and what might be triggering us. What are we trying to distract ourselves from? Sometimes the answer is obvious. Work is stressful. The boss yelled again. But other times there doesn't seem to be an obvious trigger. Sometimes we drink to avoid anything unpleasant or stressful. This experiment offers us the option to switch from seeing stress as a reason to drink to seeing it as an opportunity to be creative and find other ways to deal with our problems. Maybe addressing the source of the stress is a good idea. Maybe blowing off steam on the driving range or at a boxing gym would be equally satisfying, and you could get a healthy workout in as a bonus.

As adults, we develop all sorts of coping mechanisms to handle stress. Maybe you like to read a book, meditate, knit, watch TV, or exercise. When I was in New York, I used to go for a long run at the end of the day. Then when I was encouraged to attend all sorts of boozy work events, from happy hours to networking meetings, that healthy habit got replaced by alcohol. Over time, all my healthy coping mechanisms were replaced with alcohol, and my life was thrown completely out of balance. What I've learned is that when we're tired, stressed out, cranky, or upset, we don't need alcohol. What we need is to change our emotional state. We need to do something to go from tired to energized, from cranky to happy. And we turn to alcohol.

You are going to experience stress over the next 30 days, I can pretty much guarantee it. But rather than saying, "Screw it!" and giving up, stop and think through it. If you have a drink now, how will that make you feel later? It might make you feel better temporarily, but you'll probably feel even worse the next morning when you realize you broke your promise to yourself. But here is the thing—every day that you read a chapter, you are learning, and so I strongly encourage you to pick up right where you left off and keep going. If you make it 30 days with just a few drinks, that is a huge improvement, and you will have learned so much. This experiment is about getting through all the information and staying curious about your behavior, whatever it is. I recommend keeping a journal (you can even jot down your thoughts in the notes app on your phone) or a video diary to record your thoughts each day. Notice how your body feels physically and emotionally. You might be surprised by the changes you see from day to day.

I'm not here to tell you to stop drinking. Or to keep drinking. I'm simply here to provide you with a framework to discover your truth through logical reasoning based on scientific information. At the end of the day, you are the only one who can make the choice. My only goal is to challenge some of the beliefs that might be holding you back. It's a terrible feeling to want something new or different and feeling like you're stuck, unable to move toward it in any meaningful way. One way or another, you'll be able to make a move by the end of this experiment. Your job is simple. Observe and become aware for 30 alcohol-free days. Be a reporter. Just the facts, ma'am.

If you're used to beating yourself up over your drinking, give yourself a break during the experiment. And if you slip up, give yourself a break then, too. The goal is not to be perfect. The goal is simply to test out a new way of thinking and behaving to see how it feels. To see if it moves you closer to those desires you have for a new life. In fact, imperfection can be a wonderful tool to help you see yourself even more clearly.

What I ask of you now, for the next 30 days, is to keep an open mind. Consider the possibilities presented in each day's reading. Is it possible that you could have the facts all wrong? For example, could anxiety be a heavy influence on your drinking? Is it possible that there is more going on with marketing and the profit engine of the alcohol industry than you currently realize? Is there something going on within the brain that makes alcohol seem more attractive than it truly is? Again, all I ask is that you keep an open mind. At the end, you might decide to keep drinking, and maybe you'll naturally cut down on the amount you drink. Or you might decide to stop altogether because you feel so good. It's your body, your mind, and your choice.

▌ A FEW TIPS BEFORE YOU START

One of the most interesting things I've found in my years of research is just how many people want to change their drinking. I thought I was alone. I thought I was the only one who was questioning my drinking habits. Nothing could be further from the truth! It's not that we are alone. In our society, questioning our relationship with alcohol is a taboo, even among our closest friends. An honest conversation around drinking seems to invite judgment. Yet the statistics are staggering. Eighty percent of Americans drink alcohol, and a huge majority drink it regularly. And think about this: Out of the people you know who drink alcohol regularly, how many of them have said something like "I overdid it last night" or "After last night I am never drinking again" at one time or another? Most of them, right? Almost everyone I know, and certainly everyone I drank with, has told me that they wanted to change their drinking at some point, to some degree.

So you are not alone in wondering about this topic. You are in the vast majority.

Another thing I've realized after reaching hundreds of thousands of people with this message is that drinking more than you want is not a weakness. If you've tried to stop drinking in the past and failed, I want you to know it's not your fault. Some of the smartest and most successful people in the world drink more than they want to, including lawyers, doctors, corporate executives, psychiatrists, professors, you name it. And when they try to cut back, they don't find it easy. And when it is not easy, we blame ourselves, believing there is something wrong with us. As you will discover, there is nothing wrong with you; it's simply that you are a human being who is drinking a substance that is addictive to human beings.

Why is this happening to even the smartest and best of us? Because we're going about it all wrong. The entire conversation around alcohol is flawed. And by the time you finish this book, and the 30-day experiment, you'll see that it's not black-and-white. You're not either "a normal drinker" or "an alcoholic." Most of us fall somewhere in the middle. So relax and let go of your anxieties. There are no judgments here. And even though I've decided to stop drinking indefinitely, you might make a different decision after doing this experiment. My only goal is to give you as much truthful information as I can so that you can make the right decision for you. An *informed* decision.

▍WHAT TO EXPECT OVER THE NEXT 30 DAYS

Magic happens in 30 days. It's a period of time when the brain can actually change—by making new neural connections—to build great new habits or to eliminate habits that have held you back. But to experience that magic, you may have to deal with a few side effects. After all, alcohol is a toxin and your body needs to cleanse itself. You might experience some cravings and irritability at first. This is completely normal and will pass as the alcohol leaves your system. It takes about a week for the body to detoxify itself, so be gentle with yourself during this period. Once your system is clean, you're going to feel amazing! You'll have more energy. Your brain will feel like a fog has lifted. And it's possible you'll feel happier than you have in a long time. Here are a few things you can do to help the process along.

- **Make a firm decision to commit to this experiment 100 percent.** One firm decision takes all the stress out of the thousands of smaller decisions you have to make every day. You want to burn the boats here like there's no going back. It's only 30 days. And at the end, you get to make the final decision about whether you continue on alcohol-free.

- **Tell someone you trust about what you're doing and why.** It's okay if you don't want to announce it to the world quite yet. But there's incredible power in having someone you can confide in. Do this and you're much more likely to follow through with the whole 30 days.

- **Drink plenty of water to flush out all the toxins in your system.** The more you drink clean, pure water, the faster your body can cleanse itself.

- **Get lots of sleep.** Your body repairs itself when you're asleep, so give it all the time it needs. If you're worried you won't be able to sleep without drinking, we'll cover that later in the book.

- **Get some exercise.** You'll feel better when you get your blood moving. And I've found vigorous exercise to be a great way to overcome both cravings and irritability.

- **Eat healthy foods, especially protein.** Your body needs protein to make amino acids, which help elevate your mood.

- **Start a journal.** You're going to want to "talk" through what you learn in this book, and a journal is a great place to record your thoughts privately. You can use an app on your phone, make a video diary, or use good old-fashioned pen and paper. If you sign up at alcoholexperiment.com, you'll get a private daily digital journal. It's a great way to keep track of your amazing progress.

- **Take a photo and weigh yourself.** You might be surprised at the differences you see in your physical appearance after 30 days without alcohol.

- **Stay social.** Now is not the time to isolate yourself or lock yourself away from your friends and family. You need your social life. You need your friends. You might be nervous about going out to places where you regularly drink. But this is an experiment. You have to get out there and try it. You are experimenting with how your real life will be without alcohol. As you go along, you will be amazed to realize you don't need alcohol to socialize or have a good time. You only thought you did. Think back to when you were a child or in high school—did you need alcohol then? Weren't you having the most fun? And what's the worst that can happen? You go out to happy hour, you order a refreshing glass of iced tea, and you have a miserable time. So what? It's just one evening, and it's all part of the experiment. That is great data. You can examine exactly why you had a miserable time and whether the lack of alcohol is truly the reason. I bet you will surprise yourself by having an amazing time.

- **Be positive!** Many people tell me their biggest fear is they don't think they can do it. They aren't sure they're strong enough to make it 30 days. Don't kick off this experiment by feeling sorry for yourself. You have so much to look forward to. Sure, the cleansing process takes a little while and it's not entirely pleasant, but you are strong and you can handle it. The same people who thought they couldn't do it write to me after a week or two to say they can't believe the difference in themselves. They now know they are stronger than they thought.

- **Join this book's online social challenge at alcoholexperiment.com.** There you can do this experiment with thousands of like-minded people from all over the globe. You will get amazing community support, plus daily video resources and a private online journal to document your progress. There are even Alcohol Experiment mentors there who've already gone through this process and who are committed to helping you make it all the way to the end. (For a reader's discount, please visit alcoholexperiment .com/reader) Throughout this book, you'll find stories and observations from actual community members. The comments are real, though the names have been changed.

This is a 30-day experiment, right? So I just want you to read the short lesson for each day. Try to read it in the morning, if you can, and put the recommendations into practice during the day. Don't be surprised if you find yourself having epiphanies in the shower or shouting, "Holy cow!" while you're driving. Once your mind starts mulling over some of these ideas, there's no telling where your thoughts can go.

As with almost everything in life, your perspective can determine your outcome. So instead of thinking about giving something up, think about what you're going to gain: self-respect, more money in your wallet, a better relationship with your spouse and your kids, better health, better working relationships, a leaner body, and more.

This is exciting! You are embarking on an amazing journey. And don't worry—it's only 30 days. You can do anything for 30 days.

Are you ready?

Let's go!

▌DAY 1 ▌

What's Your Why?

The best day of your life is the one on which you decide your life
is your own. No apologies or excuses. No one to blame. The gift
is yours—it is an amazing journey—and you alone are responsible
for the quality of it. This is the day your life really begins.
—BOB MOAWAD

We've talked about how you've been unconsciously conditioned to
believe alcohol is a vital part of life for relaxing, socializing, and everything in between. And you know there are competing desires inside
your mind. Your conscious mind wants to drink less, or even stop
drinking completely. And your subconscious mind believes you need
to keep drinking for some very good reasons. Before we dive into
those beliefs and stories and deciding if they're true, we need to know
what those beliefs actually are. After reading literally thousands of
stories from people who've gone through this process, I'm pretty sure
I know what your beliefs are. But that's not important. What's important is that YOU know what they are. So let's start this experiment
by writing a list.

WHY DO YOU DRINK?

Write down a list of every reason you drink. There's no judgment here. We simply want a list.

To get you going, here's a look at part of my list. You might have some of the same reasons.

- Work is stressful and drinking helps me relax after a long day.
- Drinking helps me be more creative on the job.
- Drinking helps me be more outgoing at networking events.
- Drinking is important to my social relationships.
- I love the taste of wine.

Don't stop with a few reasons; keep going until you can't think of any more. You might come up with 50 or 100 reasons, and that's fine.

You've brought your subconscious beliefs up to the surface of your mind. Now we can shine a light on them, examine them, and you can decide for yourself whether those beliefs are true. And you can make that decision based on the facts, not social conditioning from the media and your peers. Don't do anything with this list right now. Don't try to change your mind. At the moment, these are your beliefs, and they're currently true in your life. As I present you different ideas over the next 30 days, you may think about this list differently.

WHY THE ALCOHOL EXPERIMENT?

Okay, next I want you to pull out another piece of paper and make a second list. Write down all the reasons you want to take part in this experiment. WHY do you think you might want to drink less? Here's a peek at my list:

- I'm tired of waking up slightly hungover.

MY health.

- I no longer want to worry that I said something stupid the night before.
- I am sick of the internal dialogue about my drinking—I am tired of thinking about drinking.
- I saw a photo of myself out with friends and my teeth looked purplish from wine—it was disgusting.
- I look back on certain days and my memories are so fuzzy. I am afraid I am missing my life because I can't clearly remember it all.

TODAY, read over both your lists and notice how they are in conflict with each other. This is the whole source of your cognitive dissonance. It's the battle going in your mind all the time, written in your own words. Over the coming weeks, it might help you to picture these lists on either side of a seesaw or a balance. Right now, the first list might be longer than the second one. In a few weeks, check back in to see if the balance has shifted at all.

Day 1 Reflections from alcoholexperiment.com

"I am sick of alcohol damaging my life in so many ways, including making an idiot of myself, hangovers, feeling violently ill, wasted time and opportunity, horrendous fights with my husband, putting a strain on my marriage, weight gain, no exercise, loosened stomach, way too big an appetite, anxiety, smoking, money, no time." —JULIANNA

"Today is the first day of the rest of my life." —BRIAN

"Hey guys. Day 1 here. Interested to see if my list of reasons why I drink was smaller than my list of reasons why I am here. I am taking that as a sign that I have more reason to stop than to continue drinking. I have more to gain from being AF [Alcohol Free]. I feel quite motivated by that." —ROMERO

"I decided that my life is my own and I am ready to live it the way I want to, and that doesn't include alcohol." —LIZA

||| ACT #1 |||

The Taste of Alcohol

NOTE: The idea of the ACT Technique—Awareness, Clarity, Turnaround—is to give you an alternate perspective. It is an exercise to help you resolve your or internal disagreement around alcohol. First, we'll become aware by naming a belief you have about drinking. Then we'll gain clarity around that belief, looking at where it came from and how you may have picked it up without even knowing it. We'll also look at the internal and external evidence that supports that belief (or doesn't). Finally, we'll decide if the belief holds true through a turnaround. We will look at the opposite of the belief, and decide if the opposite is as true as or truer than the original belief. When this process is complete, you get to decide if you still believe this and, more important, if that belief is serving you or if your life would be better by simply letting it go. No matter what you decide, you will gain a new perspective. The whole idea is to play detective and look at the evidence and form an objective opinion.

What's your all-time favorite drink? The one you can't wait to get your hands on at the end of a long day or on Friday night? I bet if you think about it hard enough, you can even taste it right now. Taste is an innocent reason for drinking. After all, no one thinks twice about eating ice cream or nachos. They taste good! And our favorite alcoholic beverages are the same way. But for the sake of this experiment, let's dig a little deeper.

| AWARENESS

Many people tell me they really like the taste of their favorite drink. I get it. I was a red wine girl all the way. Maybe you're a margarita lover. Or maybe you enjoy the taste of a good scotch on the rocks. Let's name this belief:

"I drink for the taste."

I know a woman who drinks a shot of Baileys in her coffee every morning before she drives her child to school. She doesn't think it's a big deal. It's just a shot, and nothing else makes her coffee taste as good. Her concerned husband tried to get her to try Baileys-flavored coffee creamer, but she insists it doesn't taste the same. But if you think about it, she's not actually tasting a lot of alcohol—it's mostly the flavorings, cream and sugar. So what do you think? Is she truly enjoying Baileys for only the taste? Or is there something else going on?

| CLARITY

In order to gain clarity around your beliefs, you need to look back at the past and figure out why you have this belief in the first place. Where did it come from? There are no right or wrong answers here, and everyone is different. So ask yourself, what observations and experiences have you had in your past that might have made you believe alcohol tastes good? Maybe it's something as simple as watching your parents pour themselves a drink at the end of the day. Or observing how they drank glass after glass in the evening. Why in the world would they drink it all the time if it tasted so bad? They're smart, right? They're grown-ups. So it must taste good, or they wouldn't keep drinking it.

I have a friend from France whose parents made sure she drank a little wine with dinner from the time she was eight years old. She hated how it tasted, and told her parents so frequently. But they continued to press on, saying she would appreciate the taste when she got older. The implication was that when she became more mature and grown-up, she would enjoy the taste of wine. We all want to appear more grown up when we're kids, don't we? Sure enough, over time my friend became a great wine lover and now drinks it every night.

Think back to your first drink and remember the experience. What were you drinking? Maybe it was wine at dinner when you were young. Maybe it was champagne on New Year's Eve when you were allowed to stay up until midnight for the first time. Maybe you snuck into your parents' liquor cabinet with a friend on a dare. Or maybe it wasn't until much later—maybe your first beer was in college. Regardless of when it was, think back to your first sip. Did you actually like it? Or did you choke and sputter, maybe even spit it out?

Who was with you at the time? Was it a friend you wanted to impress? Was it a parent you wanted to make proud? Were you trying to find a place to fit in with a new group of people? If you're like the vast majority of people I talk to, your first experience tasting alcohol was not pleasant. You didn't like it. But someone was there to say, "Don't worry, it's an acquired taste. You'll get used to it."

So take a few minutes to write down where your taste for alcohol came from. What was it like the first time you tried a new beer or hard liquor? Was it always an amazing taste you immediately loved? Did you acquire the taste over time? Or did you fake liking it because you wanted to impress someone?

Now that you have an idea where your beliefs came from, let's play detective and look at the internal and external evidence. This evidence will help you decide whether your belief that you like the taste of alcohol is true or whether you have been fooling yourself.

People have some pretty intense reactions when they taste alcohol for the first time. They talk about it burning on the way down. They wrinkle up their nose because it doesn't even smell good. Their eyes start watering. They might even spit it out. Why? One of the major reasons we don't like the taste of something is because it's harmful to us. We don't like the taste of rotten food because it can make us sick. Well, what's going on when you have a hangover? You're sick! Our taste buds react negatively to alcohol to protect us from a harmful substance.

Let's think about the idea of acquiring a taste for something. Whatever your drink of choice is, you probably didn't like it immediately. But your body allowed you to get used to it. Why? Because your brain assumes you have no choice in the matter. If you did, it would make no sense for you to keep drinking. So your body does the logical thing—it makes it easier for you to deal with the taste. You acquire it. Which, if you think about it, is the same thing as becoming immune to alcohol.

Let's look at it another way: My brother has a goat farm, and whenever I walk into the barn, there's an intense, unpleasant odor. As my sister-in-law says, it smells "very goaty." But guess what? My brother and his family don't even notice the smell anymore. Because they've gotten used to it. They have to go into the barn to feed the goats, so their brains no longer register the odor. That doesn't mean they like it. But they have, over time, gotten used to it.

If you did happen to love the taste of your first drink, it was probably something fruity or creamy that was more sugar than anything else. Am I right? Some drinks go down more easily than others. Straight alcohol is ethanol. The same stuff you put in your gas tank! A few sips will make you vomit and a few ounces of pure ethanol will kill you. I think it's safe to say you would never go suck on the end of a gas pump nozzle because it tastes good! No matter what your favorite drink is, the alcohol makes up only a small percentage of the liquid. The rest is flavorings, sugar, carbohydrates, and other additives.

Now of course there are things we appreciate as adults that we did not appreciate as children. We clearly grow a more refined palate as we age, but let's not kid ourselves: If we were purely drinking for the taste, we could certainly find other substitutes that are similar and wouldn't cause any of the side effects alcohol causes. I am intolerant to gluten and I've managed to find plenty of substitutes that aren't exactly the same but are now a natural part of my life and don't create the stomach pain gluten does. The fact is ethanol doesn't taste good. Consider this: When scientists want rats or mice to drink alcohol for a study, they have to force-feed them because they will not naturally opt to drink it.

So are you honestly drinking it for the taste?

If not, then why *are* you drinking it?

You've almost certainly observed characters in the movies and on TV enjoying the taste of alcohol, or giving a satisfying burp and a smile after chugging a beer. Even if the actors are actually drinking whiskey-colored tea, the message still gets across—it tastes good. We all tend to choose our alcohol to match our identities. If we're refined and classy, maybe we drink red wine. Or if we like old cowboy movies, maybe we lean toward whiskey. Of course, if you're an international spy, you've got to order a martini—shaken, not stirred. We identify with the characters and tend to like the same drinks they like. I used to love chugging Guinness and was so proud of my chugging ability. It made me feel tough and like "one of the boys" in that masculine work environment.

Maybe you see yourself as a discerning wine lover, and your cellar has become a status symbol. If that's the case, you probably pride yourself on your ability to discern the toasty-smoky-oaky flavors with their fruity or floral overtones. Or whatever. Here's a fun fact—the American Association of Wine Economists conducted a study of more than 6,000 wine drinkers. In this blind taste test, they discovered that people cannot tell the difference between cheap wine and expensive wine. In fact, most people preferred the taste of the cheaper varieties. And you know what else? The same blind research later found that people can't tell the difference between pâté and dog food!

So what about the argument, "alcohol enhances the taste of my food"? Do we say that about any other beverage-and-food combination? People say milk enhances the taste of cookies, but could that be because we physically dip cookies into milk? No one dips their steak into their wineglass. The truth is, alcohol is actually an anesthetic. It numbs our ability to taste, making it more difficult to savor our food.

Imagine we could remove all the physical and emotional effects of alcohol. If it couldn't actually make you drunk, would people still drink it? There's a body of pretty convincing research suggesting they wouldn't. It tastes bad. It's poisonous. Drinking for the taste is a convenient, innocent excuse. At the end of the day, is it a possibility that there's something more going on with your drinking than just the taste? Humans are incredibly adept at lying to themselves and believing their own stories. It's possible that you actually do love the taste of a cool, frosty margarita. But is it really the alcohol you like? You may not have tried a delicious virgin margarita, but the truth is, they taste as good, maybe even better! And you'll be surprised and empowered by how much you enjoy yourself without the tequila—or the hangover.

❚ TURNAROUND

This may be the most important part of the ACT Technique. Here you want to dig into the turnaround, or the opposite of the belief. You'll want to take the time to come up with as many ways as you can (at least three) that the turnaround is as true or truer than the original belief. In this case, the opposite of "*I drink for the taste*" is "*I don't drink for the taste*" or maybe even "*I don't like the taste.*" Now it's your turn to come up with as many ways as you can that the turnaround is true in your life.

▌DAY 2 ▌

It's Not What You Give Up,
But What You GAIN

One reason people resist change is because they focus on
what they have to give up, instead of what they have to gain.
—RICK GODWIN

As a participant in this experiment, you're obviously giving something up. You're giving up alcohol for 30 days. But there are two ways to look at it. You could focus on how hard it's going to be and all the things you're going to have to give up and go without. Or you could think about all the amazing insights and experiences you're going to gain as a result of the experiment.

We all undoubtedly control our destinies through our expectations. In other words, we get what we expect. If we expect this experiment to be miserable, then that is what we're going to get. And so to make this a more pleasant experience, we have to change our thinking. We have to *expect* to go into this and experience 30 days of amazing epiphanies, better health, higher energy levels, and systematic shifts in our thinking. How do we do it? We decide to focus on the positive. It's that simple. You might feel weird at first focusing on all the good things that are going to happen, especially if you're skeptical that they will happen. But when you shift your thinking to what you will gain, the good things will come. They truly will.

▌ BENEFITS

For me, I lost 13 pounds in the first 30 days. My marriage has never been better, and I've finally started doing all the things I'd wanted to do for years and years. Things alcohol kept me from doing, such as starting a business, writing a book, creating a mindfulness practice, and building a strong family life. I've become much happier socially because I'm never worried about what I said the night before. I've become much more successful. I think I look significantly better—my eyes are clearer, my hair is thicker. But these are my stories. What about other people who've gone through the 30-day experiment? What have they gained? Here's a short list from other Alcohol Experiment participants:

- Clearheaded mornings
- Better health
- Less anxiety
- True relaxation
- Better relationships
- Self-love
- Happier family life
- Freedom to fully participate in life

▌ PAY ATTENTION TO YOUR LANGUAGE

So how, exactly, do you focus on the positive? The easiest way to do it is to pay attention to your language, the words coming out of your mouth. Saying something like "I can't drink" is pretty negative. It sends all the wrong messages to your subconscious because it leaves you feeling deprived and thinking about something you can't do. On the other hand, saying "I'm going to enjoy drinking an iced tea tonight" or "I really love this lemonade" is saying the same thing in a different way. You're telling yourself you're not going to drink alcohol, but you're doing it in a positive way. And you're giving your subconscious the message that you're going to *enjoy* what you're going to do instead of that you're deprived or you can't.

Saying "I'm giving up alcohol for the month" also sends a negative message to your subconscious. But saying "I'm experimenting to see how much better I feel" is totally different. Positive phrasing sends all the right messages and will help you be more successful. So start to be mindful and conscious of how you talk to yourself.

You don't *have to* do this experiment. You *get to* do it. You have the opportunity to do this. You are excited to do this. You are *choosing* to participate. Recognize your old, disempowering, words around alcohol and replace them with new, empowering, words. This is important. The brain loves anything that gets you out of pain and into pleasure. It loves that shift both consciously and subconsciously, so choose the words you want to use. When you start consciously choosing your words, you'll even start to get a little buzz, especially if you reinforce your statements afterward. If you say, "I'm going to enjoy some iced tea tonight," reinforce it by actually feeling it. "Wow, I did enjoy that iced tea tonight!" The brain will latch on to the experience and repeat it more easily the next time.

Labeling

Another type of language you'll want to pay attention to is how you're labeling yourself and others. There's a ton of research showing how labels can limit your experience. When we put a label on something, we create a corresponding emotion based on our beliefs and experiences. That's especially true when we label ourselves and say we're depressed or we're alcoholics. It's true that we might be suffering, but by labeling ourselves that we *are* those things, we ingrain the negative feelings and end up believing them subconsciously.

It might take a little while to start catching yourself focusing on the negative or unnecessarily labeling yourself, so keep at it. If you catch yourself once a day, it's a great start. Over time you'll get better and better at it, and you'll develop ways to reprogram your language and be more positive naturally. Don't be surprised if people start noticing and telling you how much happier and upbeat you seem. That's because you *are* happier and upbeat when you expect to be and use language to reinforce the idea.

The Power of Positive

Staying positive is one amazing tool you can use to stay alcohol-free for the next few weeks, and beyond if you choose. Positive thinking and believing in yourself are helpful, but I'm also talking about how you use words in sentences. Psychologists have studied how our brains process negative statements and found that the way a sentence is constructed affects brain activity. Negative constructions can cause higher levels of activity, which means we have to think harder.

Let's keep this easy, okay? If we don't have to think hard about drinking, the experiment will be less stressful.

So, say someone asks you, "Would you like a drink?"

You could answer in the negative: "No, thanks. I'm not drinking tonight."

Or you could answer in the positive: "Yes! I'd love a club soda with lime."

By speaking with positive statements, your subconscious mind isn't triggered into activity. It's happy. It believes you enjoy drinking, and so you're enjoying a drink. It just happens to be a nonalcoholic drink this time.

How We Talk Changes Our Experiences

Furthermore, according to Albert Ellis, one of the fathers of modern psychology, how we talk about what is happening to us and around us actually changes our emotions around our experiences! One of the most powerful things I want you to learn in this experiment is that you are much more in control of your life than you may realize. Sure, it takes practice and awareness to begin to shape our emotions and experiences through our language—specifically the language we use when speaking to ourselves—but, wow, is it worth it!

I honestly can't believe the changes that have happened inside me once I learned the importance of how I talk to myself—the words I use and even the tone. Do yourself a favor: Over the next few days, start to pay attention to how you speak to yourself. Ask yourself if you would speak to a stranger like that? What about someone you consider a friend? What about your child?

Listening to Your Inner Voice

You may find it hard to "hear" your inner voice. If that's the case, do this—notice your emotions. When you start to feel anxious, upset, or stressed (or any other negative emotion), use that as a signal to pause and reflect on what you were just saying to yourself.

How we speak to ourselves has a huge impact on our emotions. This is true not only around drinking but in all areas of our lives. Studies show that the majority of most people's thinking is negative and self-destructive. However, since our inner dialogue is constant, we are not often aware of it. The next time you start to feel badly about yourself, I want you to stop and notice the words you just said inside your head. Write them down. And then ask yourself, Was it nice? Was it helpful? Was it something you would say to someone you love? Was it even something you would say to a complete stranger, or are you talking to yourself in a more destructive way than you would talk to a complete stranger? Take time every day to listen to your inner dialogue and consciously try to speak to yourself with respect. Like any habit, how you speak to yourself is unconscious, and it will take some conscious awareness to discover exactly what that inner dialogue consists of. But if you can learn to speak to yourself as you would speak to someone you love, your entire life can change for the better.

TODAY, observe your language patterns—both what you say out loud and the self-talk in your head (we'll get into even more about self-talk later in this book). And write down the words you're using on a piece of paper. Do you use the same words over and over? Are they negative or positive? When you think about alcohol, do you feel sorry for yourself and tell yourself you are not able to drink? Or do you feel excited about the challenge and tell yourself you don't *have* to drink—and don't have to wake up with another hangover? How are you treating yourself internally? Are the things you are saying to yourself generally helpful or hurtful? Will they help make these 30 days a more pleasant experience? Don't judge yourself for using negative language. Instead, think of some ways you can turn your language around and make it more positive. Make it a fun exercise.

Day 2 Reflections from alcoholexperiment.com

"My mind-set has definitely changed. Everyone around me is still drinking, and waking up with a hangover. This morning when I woke up I found myself wondering, 'Why would they do that to themselves? Why?' Then I remembered, 'Oh, yeah, I used to do that to myself, too.' It was so strange truly not being able to comprehend why people would purposefully ingest poison knowing that they would wake up feeling like shit!" —CARL

"I'm feeling great without alcohol! New things have opened up for me—some simple things like planting a little garden, trying a different grocery store, exercising more. I've already lost weight, and I never have to worry about how much I'll embarrass myself while drinking. I feel more present with my children and am not forgetting as much, or having to constantly remind myself of things I said I'd do with them." —ARLETTA

"I feel a change happening inside me, and I feel confident in myself again, or maybe for the first time. I feel like there is hope for the future and that there is so much to learn and ways in which I can grow and simply experience being human." —MORGAN

▌DAY 3 ▌

Why We Think We Like to Drink

True happiness comes from gaining insight and growing
into your best possible self. Otherwise all you're having
is immediate gratification pleasure—which is fleeting
and doesn't grow you as a person.
—KAREN SALMANSOHN

Clearly, we must like drinking. Otherwise we wouldn't do it, right? At least, in the beginning we liked it. Right now, you might be struggling with how much you actually hate the aftereffects. But there's no denying that the first drink feels good. Before we can unpack all the complicated pieces of the alcohol puzzle, it's important to understand what's actually happening in the brain when we drink.

So, I'm out with my friends, and I order a glass of wine. I've had a hard day at work, and I'm looking forward to relaxing and laughing with people I love. That first glass makes me feel giggly, and there's a little rush of euphoria that makes me feel good, maybe for the first time all day. What's happening is that the wine artificially stimulates the area of my brain called the nucleus accumbens, or the pleasure center. The chemicals responsible for euphoria are endorphins, the same chemicals responsible for the good feelings when you exercise.

❙ DOPAMINE AND SEROTONIN

Two main chemicals work in the pleasure center: dopamine, which is responsible for desire and craving; and serotonin, which is responsible for the feelings of satiety and inhibition. In a healthy brain, there is a delicate balance between the two. But alcohol throws off that balance, and so as I'm drinking that glass of wine lots of dopamine gets dumped into my system, making me want more of what gave me pleasure (the alcohol). Since the pleasure center has been artificially stimulated by an outside substance, my brain seeks to regain the correct balance. So it sends out a chemical downer, called dynorphin. This actually suppresses my feelings of euphoria, and as the effects of the first glass start to wear off, my sense of well-being actually falls *below* where it was when I started drinking. That means I'm *lower* than when I got off work after a hard day. Bummer.

The dopamine is still working, though, and makes me crave more of what made me feel good. So I order another glass of wine. And the cycle starts all over again. An unwanted effect is that in order to combat the depressant effects of alcohol, my body counteracts the alcohol by releasing things like adrenaline and cortisol. You may have heard of cortisol—it is also known as the "stress hormone." So now in my body's attempt to maintain homeostasis and combat the alcohol, I am lower than when I started. In other words, I now have to cross an even bigger gap to get above that baseline of pleasure. And that's miserable. Even worse, though, is that the alcohol is starting to affect other areas of my brain. My senses are being numbed, and my brain is actually slowing down. Eventually, I might slur my speech. Perhaps my vision blurs. I feel detached from reality. I convince myself that this is a welcome break from the real world.

The Cycle Continues

The drinking cycle continues, and I get more and more drunk. What was at first a nice tipsy feeling is now completely out of control. But I don't care because my brain isn't processing the long-term meanings and implications of my behavior. Eventually, if I'm drinking a lot, it's been slowed down so much that I have to work hard to walk straight on my way to the restroom.

My brain receptors have become numb, and my senses don't relay the information as well, and so memories aren't formed. I don't completely recall the embarrassing things I say or do while I'm drunk. I don't feel the pain I'm trying to escape. The stress from the workday fades away for a little while. But the stress remains when I sober up, and it's compounded by the hangover I'm suffering from. The embarrassing photos show up on Facebook. And my best friend won't talk to me because I pissed her off so badly . . . somehow . . . I'm not really sure what happened.

If you're reading this book, you know what I'm talking about. The initial rush doesn't last. The more drunk you get, the more you regret it when you sober up. It's a downward spiral. And if you're like me, you blame yourself. *Why can't I get it together? Why am I so weak? What's wrong with me?*

TODAY, realize that the cycle has nothing to do with you being strong or weak. It has nothing to do with you being a good or bad person. It's a chemical chain reaction that happens to everyone. Although we all feel the effects slightly differently based on our age, weight, sex, and environment, the biological reactions are the same.

Day 3 Reflections from alcoholexperiment.com

"This is my third day and already I feel like I slept better. I woke up happy that I finally committed myself mentally. It is a shift I have a hard time explaining or putting my finger on. I am embracing the idea that I do not need to hit rock bottom. It is hard to break that way of thinking, but I believe in my heart now that is true. I can quit right now, feel better right now, and not drink again. It is that simple. An aha moment!"　　　　　　　　　　　—MONICA

"I had a situation last night that would typically send me straight to the bottle or a six-pack of beer. I won."　　　　　　　　　　　—BRADY

"This is the first Saturday in as long as I can remember when I haven't woken up hungover and miserable. I am anxious, which feels like a craving, but I recognize that it is because I have so much time on my hands. What shall I do? I'm going to need to get some hobbies!"　　　　　　　　—PENNY

||| ACT #2 |||

Alcohol and Sleep

| AWARENESS

When I started researching this book, I sent out a survey asking people what their biggest fears were about giving up alcohol. I was surprised to see sleep come up high on the list. It's a huge fear for people that they won't be able to fall asleep or they won't be able to stay asleep. Let's name this belief:

"I need alcohol to sleep."

If you're struggling with this belief, you're definitely not alone. One of my favorite authors, William Porter, who wrote *Alcohol Explained*, is well versed in alcohol's effects on sleep, and he explains this topic brilliantly. So let's dig into this belief a little deeper.

| CLARITY

I'm not sure how much the media is responsible for this particular belief. There's not a lot of insomnia portrayed in the movies or on TV. However, if you've ever had a bout of sleeplessness, you know how disconcerting it can be. Sleep is critical to our mental and physical well-being. And when you can't sleep, you'll do anything to be able to fall asleep. Lack of sleep has been linked to serious health problems, including cancer, heart disease, type 2 diabetes, infections, and obesity. It also affects alertness, mood, and physical strength. This is because your body repairs itself while you sleep. It's also a time when your mind digests what happened during the day. It assimilates the information and often comes up with solutions to problems. So when you wake up, you feel better physically and mentally. That means if you've experienced alcohol helping you sleep, then this belief takes hold very quickly.

Regular, high-quality sleep is essential to our well-being. So let's look at how sleep actually works. There are two levels of sleep: rapid eye movement (REM) sleep and deep sleep, or slow-wave sleep. Every night, you go through several cycles of both levels. First, you dip into REM sleep, when you're a bit restless and your eyes are literally darting back and forth inside your eyelids (which is where the name comes from). This is light sleep, but it's crucial to your good health. Scientists don't actually know why REM is so important, but they've done studies where rats were deprived of REM sleep and it killed them in just a few weeks. Once you cycle out of REM, you go into a deeper level of slow-wave sleep. That's when the body does the repair work that needs to happen to keep you healthy. When you're getting a good night's sleep, you go through six or seven cycles of both REM and deep sleep.

Now, what happens when alcohol is introduced to the equation? Alcohol is a chemical depressant, so it reduces neural activity in the brain. Normally, your brain releases a variety of chemicals and hormones at different times to help bring you back to homeostasis. As you already know, homeostasis is the delicate balance where all the systems in your body are working correctly. When you drink, you're introducing a foreign chemical. And in order to reach homeostasis, your brain has to release powerful counter-chemicals and stress hormones.

So the cycle looks like this:

You have a drink, and you stimulate your pleasure center while the blood alcohol is rising. But as time goes on and the alcohol levels start to go down, your brain knows there's a depressant in your system. So it releases stimulants (adrenaline and cortisol) to bring you back up into homeostasis. Unfortunately, the depressant alcohol wears off before the stimulants do, and you're left with an overstimulated brain for hours after the drinks have worn off. It's as if you drank alcohol and a triple espresso at the same time. The alcohol wears off, but the espresso is still affecting you hours later.

The alcohol is disrupting your sleep schedule. After you drink, you go into a deep sleep for the first five hours or so. That might seem great, but you don't get into REM sleep. And you need both. So while your body is trying to process all the chemicals in your body, your cycles are completely thrown out of whack. You wind up with only one or two cycles of REM sleep instead of the six or seven you actually need.

After those first five hours, you wake up and can't get back to sleep. Many people wake up at three or four in the morning and fret about everything they can think of. The worry and regret creep in, and the negative thoughts take over the brain. All this is happening because you're overstimulated and your body chemistry is completely out of balance. Here's the thing—any amount of alcohol will disrupt your sleep. It doesn't matter if you have one drink or you go on a margarita binge-fest. You're not going to sleep well. If you do this night after night, the lack of quality sleep cycles will begin to take its toll.

And there's another big problem. When you start getting ready for bed without alcohol in your system, your body releases its own chemicals to quiet you down and prepare you for sleep. But when you drink regularly, you train your brain to utilize the artificial depressants in the alcohol to do that job. So that means you're relying on alcohol to put you to sleep. But you still aren't rested, because your natural sleep rhythms are out of whack.

So what does this mean for you during this experiment? It means that for the first two to five nights of not drinking, your body may still be expecting those artificial depressants. Your brain might be confused during those early days, and you could have trouble falling asleep. The worst thing you can do at that point is to have a drink to help you sleep. It might seem like the right thing to do, but it will actually set your progress back. The good news is most people find they're sleeping better than ever after the fifth night. You've given your brain time to readjust itself and get the chemical release balanced again. And once this happens, for the first time in years, or maybe decades, you will start getting the rest that your body so desperately needs. This is great news!

While you're waiting for your brain to readjust, you can try a few tricks to help you get to sleep. First, avoid caffeinated drinks after about noon. Caffeine can affect the body for up to 10 hours. So you want it all out of your system by the time you're ready to hit the sack. The other trick is to get a bit of exercise. When you get your body moving, you'll actually find you sleep much better than if you're at rest all day long. You don't have to do anything extreme. You can simply take a walk in the fresh air and get your blood moving.

If you've been drinking for a long time, you may not even notice the daily fatigue you're experiencing because of disrupted sleep patterns. You might think it's because you're "getting older." Maybe you're always tired and you tell yourself, "That's just how I am." We are so overworked and undernourished that fatigue has become completely normal. Let me give you some good news: Once you stop drinking and get your sleep regulated, that fatigue and brain fog often disappear completely. You'll feel better than you have in ages! That's your reward. But you have to get through those first few days and give your body a chance to fix itself.

▌ TURNAROUND

The opposite of "*I need alcohol to sleep*" is "*I don't need alcohol to sleep.*" Come up with as many ways as you can that the opposite is as true as or truer than the original belief.

| DAY 4 |

Dealing with Discomfort

If the only thing that people learned was not to be afraid of
their experience, that alone would change the world.
—SYDNEY BANKS

When you decide to give up alcohol, you might experience some discomfort. I am not talking about severe physical addiction here. If you've been drinking heavily for a long time, your body and mind may have become physically dependent to the point where you have severe withdrawal symptoms, such as delirium tremens or hallucinations. If that's the case, you need to get medical help. You may even need to be hospitalized for a while. When I say "discomfort," I'm talking about the physical symptoms that occur while your body is healing itself. I'm also talking about the psychological and emotional discomfort that comes up because you're giving up something you believe you need.

It takes time, up to a week or longer, for your body to rebalance after you stop drinking. While that's happening, you're probably going to feel uncomfortable. Because alcohol is physically addictive, there are withdrawal symptoms, which are different for different people. When I stopped drinking, I had headaches, anxiety, irritability, and weird nightmares that I accidentally had a drink. The first 10 days were the most intense, but the symptoms went on for about 30 days. Clearly, that's longer than the time it took for the chemical substance to clear out of my body. So, what gives? Why did it take so long? Shouldn't we feel better as soon as the alcohol is gone? Our bodies are more complicated than that, and there's an emotional side to withdrawal as well.

When researchers studied heroin addicts, they found that the severity of withdrawal could depend on the individual's access to the substance they were addicted to. For instance, if the person went to jail and suddenly had zero access to their drug of choice, the withdrawal symptoms weren't as severe as one might expect. But when that person was released years later, and they suddenly had access again, the withdrawal symptoms came back. How weird is that? How is it possible to go through withdrawal years after ingesting a substance? This demonstrates how physical and emotional withdrawals are intertwined. Each affects the other, and our subconscious can easily keep things buried for a long time and then allow them to resurface later.

CHANGING YOUR MIND-SET

What helped me get through this initial period of physical withdrawal was flipping my mind-set. Instead of seeing the headaches and anxiety as punishment for an addiction that I should have been able to control, I chose to see them as signs that my amazing body was healing itself. I was willing to be sick and put up with the discomfort to make my body whole again. I knew I had been treating it poorly. So I decided to treat it with kindness and give it whatever time it needed to heal.

If you're not feeling your best right now, cut yourself some slack. Imagine if your child was feeling sick. Would you yell at her for being a "bad person" or tell her she was "getting what she deserved"? Of course not! You'd let her rest on the couch, eat chicken soup, and maybe watch some cartoons. You'd tell her to let her body do its job. Give yourself the same courtesy.

The Emotional Aspects

As you probably know, there's more to withdrawal than physical discomfort. There's an emotional side as well. And both sides are all tangled up with each other. It's almost like as soon as you get a handle on one, the other falls to pieces and you're so tempted to give up this experiment and crack open a beer. I get it! On the emotional side, you might feel sad, angry, or resentful. After all, you're giving up something you believe you enjoy. Your subconscious believes you need alcohol to loosen up, relax, have fun with your friends, or handle stress. When you take that coping mechanism away without dealing with these subconscious beliefs, there will be consequences in the form of emotional distress and cravings.

That is why I'm calling these 30 days an "experiment." You're simply testing the waters to see how you might feel if you weren't drinking. Your subconscious mind isn't necessarily going to like that, but it's better than laying down the law and saying, "No more alcohol ever!" That kind of ultimatum can result in a full-on emotional mutiny.

Throughout the course of this experiment, you're going to explore those subconscious beliefs of yours. One day at a time, you're going to read a little bit about different ideas that might make you question what you once thought was true. By the time you reach the end of this book, in fact, you might decide that you never need or even want another drink. And your subconscious will totally go along with it. That's called spontaneous sobriety, and it happens all the time. It happened to me. When your conscious and subconscious minds are in harmony and desire the same thing, there's no cognitive dissonance. And when that happens, there's no struggle. You have no cravings and no desire to go back.

Getting Curious

But that's later. For right now, simply realize that your feelings and physical symptoms are real. Take the time to feel them. Honor them.

Appreciate what your body is trying to tell you. And do not give in to the temptation to use alcohol to numb them. These symptoms are temporary. They will go away in time.

So what can you do in the meantime? How do you handle the emotional discomfort and strong desire to give in?

My solution was to get curious about my own behavior. Anytime I had a strong urge to drink, I sat with it and went deep into what was going on. I became an internal reporter. I asked myself questions all the time to find out what I was feeling exactly and what was actually causing me to feel that way. Sometimes I felt like I was missing out because I was with a group of friends who were all drinking. Other times I'd had a hard day at work and felt like I needed a drink to calm my nerves. Other times I felt like I'd been good for so long that I "deserved" to have a drink as a reward.

TODAY, instead of trying to ignore or overcome your discomfort by having a drink, ask yourself, "Why do I want to drink *right now*? What is it that I think alcohol will do to make this moment better?" And then ask yourself, "Is that true?" If you're completely objective and honest, you might surprise yourself with your answers.

Do this little exercise first. Write down your answers, or record yourself in a video diary or voice memo. By doing this, you're observing the symptoms as something separate from you. You're giving yourself perspective—and a little bit of time for the feelings to subside. And remember that your body is amazing. It's taking care of you right now by getting rid of all the toxins it's had to deal with for a long time. Yes, you might not feel your best for a bit. But when the process is complete, your body will feel better than ever.

And consider the online social challenge at alcoholexperiment .com; you can find thousands of others who are also doing this experiment. Sharing your insights with others in a safe, judgment-free environment is incredibly powerful.

Day 4 Reflections from alcoholexperiment.com

"Good days but bad nights. Woke up at 3 a.m. not feeling the best but definitely not hungover. And a bit of a headache this morning. I spent the day thinking about all the holidays and times with my kids I don't remember. Yesterday it dawned on me how much time alcohol has stolen from me. Yes, I let it. But the reading today very much reinforced that. I am generally happy. Still thankful!"   —ROBYN

"I have been having such strange dreams, I feel such a physical difference. I didn't realize alcohol takes so long to get out of your system, so even though I binge-drink once or twice a week, I was feeling so crappy because I was never alcohol-free. I had constant headaches, fatigue, bloating, nausea. I am learning so much!"   —GEORGE

"Didn't expect the physical symptoms to be so real. Glad I understand why I am having them. Still better than being hungover. Need to be gentle on myself and others through this. Can't wait to sleep again!"   —HECTOR

| DAY 5 |

What Are Cravings, Really?

Knowledge renders belief obsolete.
—NANA JANE

I've found there are two kinds of cravings you have to contend with at different times: physical cravings and emotional cravings. Physical symptoms such as anxiety, restlessness, and the inability to sleep show up while the alcohol is still in your system. We know they're cravings because they go away if you give in and have a drink. It can take up to a week for alcohol to completely leave your system, so that's about how long you can expect those physical cravings to last. After that point, you're most likely looking at mental or emotional cravings. (Fortunately, you probably know exactly the last time you had a drink. When people try to get over a sugar addiction, they sometimes consume sugar without even knowing it because it's hidden in so many food products!)

Psychological or emotional cravings can be much harder to handle simply because they are triggered by certain circumstances that your subconscious knows (from experience) may be helped by having a drink. You've reached the point in your relationship with alcohol that it's taking more than it's giving, and you feel like you want to cut back or stop. That's a conscious decision you've made. But if your subconscious mind still believes that alcohol is key to relaxation and that you have to drink to have a good time with your friends, then those psychological cravings will creep in—sometimes years after you've had any alcohol. Your desires originate from your subconscious mind. And a craving is a desire.

CRAVINGS AND STRESS

For example, if you used to handle work stress by drinking, like I did, then every time you experience work stress, you'll likely trigger a psychological craving for alcohol. You've already wired your brain to do this. It's a learned response. Your subconscious believes drinking reduces stress, even though science has proven that alcohol actually increases stress over time. And even though you've made the conscious decision not to drink, your subconscious didn't get the memo. So it sends up a desire—a craving.

If your cravings are triggered by stress, you have to find another way to reduce that stress. Studies have shown over and over that exercise is a great way to do that. Once those endorphins get released, the stress and cravings subside. Mindfulness and meditation are other great ways to reduce stress. Don't worry, you don't have to shave your head and move to Tibet. There are all kinds of forms of meditation— all you're really doing is exercising your brain.

The Internal Battle

So you have this battle going on inside you. Your conscious and subconscious are fighting it out over whether you want a drink. It's frustrating. It's confusing. And it's tempting to try to ignore the craving or exert your willpower over it. But that rarely works. Science tells us that the more we try to repress a thought or ignore something, the harder it is to escape. It's much better to be completely present and mindful during a craving. Notice how you feel and what thoughts are running through your head when you separate yourself and become an observer watching this weird battle between your conscious and subconscious. Detach yourself from the outcome and you're less likely to give in.

I like to visualize my subconscious mind as a child riding in the backseat of a car. Suddenly the child decides he or she wants an ice cream cone and won't let it go. Children are the best salespeople in the world because they don't give up. They don't take no for an answer. They'll keep attacking the problem in a different way over and over until they get what they want.

"Can I have an ice cream, Mom?"

"That ice cream sure looks good!"

"Look! A gas station. Don't you need gas, Mom? I bet they have ice cream inside."

"What's your favorite ice cream, Mom? I like chocolate!"

"So, when are we getting ice cream? Now or after dinner?"

"You know what would make Dad happy? A surprise ice cream!"

If children think there's even the slightest chance that they'll get what they desire, they will keep pestering you. Even if you don't have kids, you've been a kid. So you know what I'm talking about, right? The only way to get children to give up is to get rid of the desire, which means either distracting them or making them understand that there is NO WAY they are getting an ice cream.

Distraction

This is how you deal with cravings, too. You can distract yourself with a book, a walk, or a dinner date. You can also substitute something that will satisfy the desire without giving in to the craving. If you need to hold a glass in your hand at a networking event, fill it with tonic water or soda. Often that's enough to satisfy your subconscious child.

But what if distraction doesn't work and you still have that craving? That means your little darling believes there's a chance you'll give in. We all know how that works with kids and ice cream, right? If you give in once, the next time they'll be even MORE relentless. It will be even harder to get them to stop nagging you. All the kid cares about is getting the ice cream, and they won't stop until they truly believe there's no way it's going to happen. Relying on willpower to resist a craving is like arguing with a child using grown-up logic.

"Sorry, honey, we don't have time to stop for ice cream . . ."

"It will spoil your dinner . . ."

"We don't have the money . . ."

"You don't need an ice cream . . ."

What kid is going to fall for that stuff? They'll come up with a counterargument every time. And they will outlast you! Eventually, they'll wear you down.

Here's something cool about your subconscious—it can produce strong desires, but it can't make you take action. It's your conscious mind that decides whether to give in.

You Have a Choice!

The more times you don't give in to your subconscious, the faster it will get the message next time. No means no. Be the parent. When your subconscious understands that you don't go back on your word, then it will believe you when you say, "Not today, honey. Maybe next week we'll get an ice cream, but for today we're going to skip it."

A good friend of mine told me about using a key phrase that got her kids to stop nagging. She said she would go into "duck mode," which meant she let whatever the child was saying roll off her like water off a duck's back. When she said, "duck mode," her kids knew there was no way they were going to get what they wanted. This is because she had never once gone into duck mode and then given in. She had taught them that duck mode meant business and that there was simply no point in arguing any longer. Because of her dedication to the tool, her kids truly believed that once she had gone into duck mode, it was in their best interest to be quiet. They knew there was no longer anything they could say that would make a difference. And so peace was restored. In my analogy of the child in the backseat of a car, the driver (your conscious mind) is in control, and the child (your subconscious mind) believes it. You can come up with a key phrase of your own—whatever works for you.

TODAY, anytime you start to crave a drink, visualize your craving as an incessant child. And then instead of getting angry or frustrated, use whatever technique gets the child to believe you're serious about your commitment. Distraction or duck mode—whatever works is great!

Day 5 Reflections from alcoholexperiment.com

"Last night my husband had a bottle of wine in the fridge. Told him to go ahead, I didn't want any. . . . There was no craving, no thoughts of missing out."   —TAMMY

"I am feeling very accomplished. I went to a Mexican restaurant today and I did not order a beer or a margarita. . . . What?! That's huge for me! Most of my poor drinking habits are triggered in social situations, and so this was a small victory for me. I love going to see live music, and there is a concert coming up in less than a month and the idea of not having a drink there is daunting. I wonder . . . will I even have fun? OMG, I feel so ridiculous for even thinking this . . . but it's the truth. I am no longer going to lie or try to cover up my thoughts around drinking. I am just going to keep shining a light on them so that eventually they will have nowhere to hide and there will be nothing left for me to be afraid of."   —TRISH

"I've struggled with my spouse's drinking for years but realize I have a problem, too, and I need to focus on myself. I love waking up feeling great! I love not 'planning' around drinking. I feel good about not being part of the problem, which I was when drinking with my spouse. Really, how can I preach moderation or quitting when I'M not moderating or quitting?"   —PEGGY

▌DAY 6 ▌

Why Willpower Doesn't Work for Long

If you don't sacrifice for what you want,
what you want becomes the sacrifice.
−ANONYMOUS

For our purposes we will specifically define *willpower* as using conscious mental energy or effort to stop doing something (like drinking) or start doing something (like exercise).

If you've ever tried to lose weight, stop gambling, or make your bed every day for a month, you've probably tried to harness willpower to get through it. Spending 30 days alcohol-free is no different. It's only 30 days, right? How hard could it be? Well, here's the deal with willpower—it's a finite and exhaustible resource. *Willpower* can also be defined as the ability to resist short-term temptations in order to meet long-term goals. Some people think it's a skill that can be honed and perfected. Or a muscle that can be built up and maintained. But it doesn't seem to work that way. New research shows it's more like an energy reserve, and when the reserve is low, there's not much you can do until you top it back up.

▌WHY WILLPOWER FLUCTUATES

Mark Muraven, an associate professor of sociology at Case Western Reserve University, wanted to understand why he had lots of willpower at certain times but not others. He conducted an experiment to prove that willpower was more effective when conserved and that, when taxed, it could run out. Subjects, under the guise that they were participating in a taste-based experiment, were placed in a room with two bowls on a table. One bowl was full of fresh-baked cookies, and the other was full of radishes. Half the subjects were told to eat the cookies and ignore the radishes, and the other half were told to eat the radishes and ignore the cookies. (Bummer for them, right?)

After five minutes both groups were given a puzzle that appeared easy but did not actually have a solution. Because the puzzle was impossible, continuing to work on it required willpower. The subjects who had previously used willpower to ignore the cookies worked on the puzzle for 60 percent less time than the subjects who had not used any of their willpower reserves. And there was a drastic difference in attitudes. The radish-eaters were grumpy and frustrated, and even snapped at the researchers.

All Decisions Take Energy

Every decision you make requires you to expend a certain amount of energy, and that includes energy you might prefer to save up for exercising willpower. If you have a hard day at work, and you've had to make lots of decisions, your energy and willpower will both be lower. This is why it's easier to resist temptation early in the day, but by the time five o'clock rolls around, you just want a martini. It's exhausting exercising your willpower all day.

There's also something called the "what the hell" effect, which explains what happens when you abandon your quest for willpower, give in to temptation, and then, since you feel badly for giving in, throw caution to the wind and end up going overboard. You slip up and drink. Regret sets in, but since you've already had one drink, you think, "What the hell—I might as well get drunk."

No matter how much willpower you started the day with, by the time happy hour rolls around, it's pretty much gone. You might be able to muster up willpower for that evening, but what about when you get home? What about the next day? And the next?

What are you going to do? Lock yourself in a closet for the rest of your life?

Clearly, willpower is not the answer as long as your cognitive dissonance around drinking remains firmly embedded in your mind. As long as there are two competing ideas—to drink or not to drink—you will struggle and expend energy trying to resist those subconscious messages using your conscious logic. But once you resolve that dissonance and are of one mind about alcohol, there is no struggle. There's no decision to make. And willpower is no longer required. You can use it for something else, like saying no to that piece of chocolate cake. (Of course, you can use the ACT Technique to take care of your chocolate cravings, too.)

TODAY, take out a small piece of paper or an index card and write down a few of the facts about alcohol that you now know to be true. *Alcohol actually increases stress in the body. When I go out with my friends, I'm happy with a tonic and lime. I don't need alcohol to have fun.* Then keep that card handy in your wallet or cell phone case. Whenever you feel yourself relying on willpower to get you through a situation, or you feel like you're about to give in, pull out the card and read it. Calming the dissonance in your mind will do more than trying to grit your way through the situation.

Day 6 Reflections from alcoholexperiment.com

"I left work thinking I wanted—and needed—a drink. My boss has been a total jerk for a few days, and it is not like him to be like that. Anyway, it's very uncomfortable. I was able to resist the drink and ride it out. And I actually feel better. Alcohol does numb my brain so I quit obsessing about all of it. I may or may not talk to him about it tomorrow, but not drinking is really my first priority. It changes everything for me. I feel better, look better, am more clearheaded, less anxious, foggy, etc. I could go on and on. Thanks, everybody, and thanks, Annie." —CARL

"Two things are going really well (probably more, but these two are delighting me at the moment). 1. I'm waking up with so much more energy and I'm channeling it into all sorts of creative projects. 2. I feel my mood lifting a little more each day, and I was convinced I'd live the rest of my life under a cloud of depression and grumpiness. I'm welcoming back my silly, quirky, goofy self. I love that version of me! She makes me smile. (And God love my husband for hanging with the cranky, grumpy version for so long. He's smiling more these last few days, too.)" —CAMMIE

"For a while now, I have been somewhat grumpy about the cognitive dissonance. I gave up alcohol for a bit after finding out more about booze, but then started again. The problem was that with my new knowledge about alcohol, I really did not enjoy drinking. I hated the hangovers and the anxiety that followed. I was even mad that by knowing more about alcohol, my drinking 'hobby,' the thing that connected me with so many people in life, had been ruined for me—so I kept drinking. But this time is different. All that seems to have gone. There is clear blue sky in my head, not storm clouds. I can confidently say no to a drink. I know there are challenges ahead, but I am feeling positive about them." —JAMES

||| ACT #3 |||

Alcohol, Relaxation, and Stress Relief

| AWARENESS

If you're drinking to relax, like I used to do, you are not alone. Relaxation and stress relief are some of the main reasons people drink. After all, who can deny that a few drinks totally relaxes you and relieves everyday pressures, stress, and anxiety? There's a reason it's called "happy hour," right? You can't use willpower to grit your way through and ignore the idea that alcohol relaxes you. Let's name this belief:

"Alcohol relieves stress and helps me relax."

We watch people in movies and on TV and all around us drinking to relax. There's a reason that happy hour starts at five o'clock. Work stresses us out. Money stresses us out. Our relationships stress us out. And stress stresses us out—it's a major contributor to many deadly diseases. For most of us, the pressures and expectations of modern living seem out of control. And we're taught to simply drink our problems away instead of facing them head-on.

| CLARITY

So why do we believe this? When in our past have we observed and experienced alcohol taking the edge off stress and anxiety? We could start with our parents and relatives. When you were young, did your mom or dad come home after a long day and immediately pour a drink? It's been part of our culture since we were children. If not yours, what about your friends' parents? We certainly all watched TV shows and movies where the dad comes home and immediately grabs a beer from the fridge. Or the homicide detectives talk over the case at a local bar. As we grew older and went to college, partying was the natural way to blow off the stress from exams or a long day of lectures. We've seen people doing this in real life, and there are numerous movies whose whole story line revolves around a huge college drunk-fest after final exams.

It's almost inevitable that we started mimicking what we observed. Everywhere we look, society is telling us that if we have to do something hard, we need a drink to cope with it. So it's pretty easy to see where this belief might have come from. Take a few minutes right now to write down some *specific instances* when you observed or experienced alcohol being relaxing. If your parents drank after work, what *exactly* did they drink? And how did they behave afterward? What specific movies or TV shows do you remember watching where a character drank to relax? Try to pinpoint how and when you started to believe that you need alcohol to relax.

Now let's look at some internal and external evidence to help you decide whether alcohol truly helps you relax. First of all, let's define *true relaxation*. What exactly are we trying to do with the stress and anxiety we may be experiencing in the moment? We're trying to get rid of it, right? True relaxation is the *absence* of stress and anxiety. It's not ignoring the stress or numbing it—real relaxation *removes it* completely. To get to that point, you must deal with the source of the stress—talk with your boss about a problem, rearrange your schedule to avoid a conflict, or whatever it is you need to do to remove the discomfort. You can't get that out of a bottle. A shot of tequila can't fix your marriage. It can only make you not worry about it for a little while.

It's true that you can equate that initial tipsy feeling with being relaxed. How long can you sustain it? Twenty minutes? An hour? Drinkers almost never feel relaxed for a full hour, because as the alcohol is metabolized, we actually feel more stress than we did when we started. Alcohol leaving the body makes us feel *worse*. So what do we do? Have another!

It's ironic that we drink to relax, because drinking actually adds stress to our lives. I'm not going to deny that alcohol definitely provides the illusion of relaxation, especially at first. But here's what's actually happening. That drink is simply numbing the senses and slowing the mind. For a short time, we truly don't care about our problems, and we feel relaxed. But we're not actually eliminating the problem or concern. Instead of solving the issue and removing it, we're actually postponing it and prolonging the pain.

Because we build a tolerance for alcohol, we need more and more of it to have the same effect, which introduces a host of other stress-inducing concerns. How much did I drink last night? Why is my wife angry with me? What embarrassing things did I do or say? How am I going to get up and go to work with this hangover? How can my bank account be overdrawn *again*? This cycle is the opposite of relaxation. It puts additional stress and strain on our health, finances, and relationships. And the more we use alcohol to numb our senses, the more alcohol we need, and the more stress we add to our lives. After a few years of regular drinking, the stress can truly become unbearable. Think about it like this: If alcohol truly relaxed us, wouldn't we need less of it over time? So why do we find we need more and more to reach the same level of relaxation? If we drink to relax on a daily basis, shouldn't it be easier, not harder, to get that relief?

Let's also take a look at the external evidence around this belief and what's actually happening neurologically when you drink. Your brain is a reactive mechanism. When you drink, it reacts to bring your body back into balance. Because alcohol is a natural depressant, your brain counteracts it by releasing stimulants, including adrenaline and cortisol. Guess what? Those are not only stimulants but also stress hormones. Cortisol is released in stressful situations and has been linked to a higher risk of infection, mood swings, high blood pressure, fat storage, and even premature aging. (Talk about added stress!) Adrenaline is linked to your fight-or-flight response, which is great if you're being chased by a lion. But in large amounts, adrenaline is also linked to insomnia, nervousness, and lower levels of immunity.

Here's where the bad news gets worse. Remember that alcohol takes about a week to completely leave your body. So if you're a regular drinker, you are in a constant state of withdrawal. Which means you have consistently elevated levels of cortisol and adrenaline. Which means you're always stressed on a physiological level. Add on the everyday stressors of work, health, and relationships, and it's no wonder you want to escape for a little while! One drink and that anesthetic takes over, decreasing your senses and slowing your brain function. The more you drink, the less you feel. And if you drink until you pass out, you get to feel absolutely nothing for a short time.

But guess what? As soon as you sober up, all those stressors will remain. And then some. You made things worse. And the longer you drink to "relax," the more the problems will pile up. And you'll become less and less capable of handling everyday complications.

Scientists studied this phenomenon with two groups of mice. One group was given alcohol over a 30-day period, and the other was not. At the end of the 30 days, they were put through extraordinarily stressful situations and their responses were measured. The mice that had consumed alcohol had a much harder time dealing with all the external stressors presented to them. The same was true for me. When I was drinking regularly, even the most mundane problems overwhelmed me. But once alcohol was no longer affecting my internal systems, I was able to handle them without a problem. I know life isn't always easy. But when you drink, you're limiting your ability to cope. Everything you do feels so much more difficult.

So what do you think? Does alcohol *really* relax you? Does it actually help you deal with stress and anxiety? Or is it simply numbing you out so you can ignore it for a little while? Understanding the root cause of your stress and removing it completely is the only way to enjoy true relaxation.

| TURNAROUND

The opposite of *"alcohol relieves stress and helps me relax"* is *"alcohol does not relieve stress and help me relax"* or *"alcohol adds stress to my life."* Come up with as many ways as you can that the opposite is as true as or truer than the original belief.

Your Experiment and Your Friends

Whenever you find yourself on the side of the majority,
it is time to reform (or pause and reflect).
–MARK TWAIN

You've been working on this experiment for a week now. Congratulations! How do you feel?

| ARE PEOPLE STARTING TO NOTICE?

At this point, some of your friends might be noticing that something about you has changed. Maybe you've been out with them and turned down a drink. Or maybe they've noticed a change in your behavior or even your physical appearance.

Sooner or later, you're going to have to tell someone about what you're doing. And sometimes your friends won't understand why you've decided to spend 30 days alcohol-free. Not only that, but they may even keep offering you drinks right through the challenge. They may say, "C'mon, it's just one. Don't be such a loser."

When people want to quit smoking, everyone around them is supportive and thinks it's great. And a friend wouldn't even think of offering a cigarette to a friend in that situation. So what makes alcohol different?

We're Often Hesitant to Tell Our Friends

You might be a little hesitant to tell even your friends, and I believe there's a pretty good reason for that. I think the crux of the problem is that we treat alcohol differently than we do any other addictive substance. For example, we don't have "cigarette-aholics" or "heroin-ism," but we do have "alcoholics" and "alcoholism." When we say "cigarette addiction" or "heroin addiction," we're talking about the addiction, not the people themselves. But the word *alcoholic* defines a person. The word itself blames the person rather than the substance.

For some reason in our culture, a heroin addict is someone to be pitied because they've been overpowered by an addictive substance. But an alcoholic is someone who was weak and unable to control themselves around something as innocent as a glass of beer. And it's no wonder we do this. According to certain statistics, 86 percent of people over 18 have drank alcohol at some point.[1] That's a huge number. And I think the only way we can justify to ourselves that so many people drink is to simply not talk about the fact that alcohol is addictive, just like heroin and tobacco are.

As a Society, We Don't Seem to Realize That Alcohol Is Addictive

We don't talk about the fact that when we party on a Friday night and end up puking, that physical reaction is our body's way of saving our life because we literally poisoned ourselves.

And so the language that's developed around alcohol, and the attitude of blaming the person instead of the substance, has created this huge taboo against talking about it at all. We treat every other substance that's bad for us differently than we treat alcohol. I might be chatting with my friend in front of a big box of doughnuts and say, "Mmmm, this is a really good doughnut! But I'll only have half because all the fat and sugar isn't good for me."

No one ever says, "Mmmm, this is a good chardonnay! But I'm just going to have one glass because I worry about the breast cancer and the liver damage." That doesn't happen. We have successfully separated alcohol out from other toxic substances. We even say "alcohol and drugs," as if alcohol weren't also a drug, in spite of the fact that alcohol kills more people every year than prescription and illegal drugs combined.[2] In fact, according to two independent studies about what is the most dangerous drug, alcohol won the prize.[3]

So, I think this societal attitude is why people treat you differently when you quit smoking or cut down on sugar. Because when you tell your friend that you're not drinking, there's an automatic implied judgment. Because that friend probably feels like they drink about the same amount as you. And if you think you're drinking too much, then you must also think *they* are drinking too much. Whether it's true doesn't matter. And guess what? They probably have some internal conflict around their own drinking, so the fact that you are *not* drinking is painful for them.

Perspective Change

When I was drinking a lot, I couldn't comprehend why anyone would choose not to drink. Why on earth not? What was the big deal? It didn't make sense to me. Looking back on those days now, I can see that deep down inside I knew I was treating my body badly. And when I was confronted with friends who'd made the decision to *stop* treating their bodies badly, it made me feel like they were strong and I was weak. I didn't like that.

And there's another reason your friends may try to sabotage your efforts. They don't want to lose you! One of the most fundamental parts of being human is that we crave community and interaction with other people. And we've given alcohol this magical power to make us all into fun-loving, laid-back party animals. I thought that without alcohol I wouldn't be any fun. I believed that alcohol was the glue that held some of my friendships together.

When I decided alcohol no longer had a place in my life, it set me apart. And humans don't like to be apart. So your friends may feel like you will ostracize them or you won't want to spend time with them anymore. Nobody wants that!

Is It Fear? Are They Afraid of Their Own Drinking?

If your friends aren't being supportive, realize it's probably out of fear. They're afraid you're judging them. Deep down, they know that maybe they shouldn't want to drink as much as they do. They may be afraid you won't want to spend time with them anymore. And they may be afraid that they might be an alcoholic. When people question their drinking, they might actually be wondering, *Am I an alcoholic?* And the implications of that seem horrific.

Alcoholism has been defined as a lifelong disease for which there is no cure. Alcoholics must completely abstain from drinking forever. They have to label themselves as alcoholics for the rest of their lives, even if they manage to stay sober. Alcoholism is portrayed as a never-ending fight for control. A fight that, if people lose, could cost them their marriage, their job, their children, or even their life. That is so scary! No one wants to think about that when all they're trying to do is unwind after a long day at work.

TODAY, plan how you can bring up the subject with those close to you so you can keep your fun, friendly relationship with them. Here are a few ideas for how to talk to your friends without alienating them:

Keep it light and joking: "I'm overdoing it on iced tea! Ha-ha."

Be self-deprecating (but not too much; you are doing an amazing thing and don't need to be apologetic): "I drank enough last month to last for the next 30 days, so I'm taking a break."

Let it lie. The truth is, the less you make of it, the less they will make of it. Sometimes we assume people are judging our behaviors when in reality people are mostly thinking about themselves. If you shrug it off like it's no big deal, they will also. I love to simply say, "I'm good, thanks. . . . By the way, I've been meaning to ask you, how have you been lately? What's new in your life?" This not only turns down a drink but also often kicks off a great conversation.

Day 7 Reflections from alcoholexperiment.com

"I can't believe I am here at Day 7. Feeling more positive and having more belief and confidence in myself. You don't realize what alcohol steals from you until you get it back. Stay strong, everyone!" —MATTHEW

"It doesn't matter what others think of my not drinking—this is my journey. But socially I am more comfortable now. Knowing I had a problem and just rode along enjoying the buzz, not paying attention to what I was doing to my body, really makes me sad. But on the other hand, it keeps me alcohol-free knowing I can't have one because it would start all over again. It is quite freeing to put this addiction behind me and cut the ties that alcohol once had on me." —TOMMY

"I'm loving this! Thank you so much, Annie, for the resource! So far I'm on Day 7, and it's been pretty easy. I think when you're changing your mind about something, you have to mentally ingest as much supportive information as possible. As for the reasons I give people I don't know very well (or feel I'll be judged by), I prefer to say that alcohol was making me depressed, so I decided to stop to feel better. It's definitely the truth! And no one can argue that alcohol isn't a depressant. This way, I feel empowered instead of disempowered by my choice. I don't choose to be labeled as an 'addict' or 'alcoholic.' If I had to find another reason to give people to remain neutral and free from judgment, I would just say that alcohol was making me feel sick, and it didn't agree with my body. That's definitely the truth!" —ZOE

How Alcohol Affects Your Senses

All our knowledge begins with the senses.
—IMMANUEL KANT

Your five senses are how your brain collects information about what's going on inside and outside your body. If there's a fire nearby, your brain needs to be able to smell the smoke, feel the heat, and hear the crackle to make decisions. It also needs to see the fire to sort out whether you've got a dangerous threat (like a nearby explosion) or you're enjoying a nice, relaxing campfire. Your senses are amazing tools.

So what happens to those tools when we drink? They are dulled and become much less effective communicators. Worse, our brains process the information more slowly. It's kind of like a video that takes forever to buffer and play on your computer. There's a lag. It might be inconvenient and cause you to say something embarrassing. Or that lag might be deadly and cause you to drive your car into oncoming traffic. Unfortunately, there's no way to know how bad the lag is until it's too late.

| WHAT HAPPENS IN THE BRAIN

Alcohol depresses the central nervous system and slows down your neurotransmitters, which are the chemicals responsible for moving information back and forth between your body and your brain. When your brain can't process the information as quickly as usual, your senses are affected. They're sitting there staring at that "buffer bar," saying, "Come on . . . come on . . . why is this taking so long?"

You know how sometimes a video never fully loads on your computer? Your brain can do that, too. That's when you pass out. But before you get to that stage, you'll notice your senses dulling. Blurred vision, slurred speech, numbness in your fingers and toes—sound familiar? Have you ever wondered why people talk louder when they're drunk? It's because their sense of hearing is impaired. Even your sense of touch is affected, as your ability to perceive pain decreases. That may seem like a good thing if you have chronic back pain, but it's not so great when you fall down and break your arm—but you can't feel it until you've done even more damage.

An Early-Warning System

Our senses keep us safe. They alert us to big dangers but also give us smaller hints when something doesn't feel quite right. In addition to being an early-warning system, they also help us experience pleasure and happiness. Did you know that one of the most arousing scents for men is pumpkin pie? Seriously, it's an aphrodisiac (which may or may not explain the popularity of pumpkin spice lattes).

Memories: One of Life's Most Precious Gifts

Our memories are also connected to our senses. When we drink, we're dulling those senses of pleasure and robbing ourselves of wonderful happy experiences. And we're robbing ourselves of the memories we should be storing. One of the reasons you don't remember the party last night is because you didn't get that sensual information stored away. Your senses were too dull and slow to store away the experience of laughing and joking with your friends, or of that first kiss you've been waiting for. Is it worth not remembering your child's birthday party because you just had to have a few glasses of wine to get through it? One of my biggest regrets is my son's third birthday party. We had this incredible party, and even looking at the photos I can't remember it. I had made sangria early and drank quite a bit of it, and no matter how hard I try to remember anything, that day is gone. The funny thing is that no one could even tell how much I was drinking, but the memories are just not there. And to this day it breaks my heart that I missed such an important day. When I think about how many things I've missed that I don't even know that I've missed—because they weren't as evident as a birthday party—I realize how much alcohol has stolen from me.

Too often, we take our senses for granted and don't realize how much we'd miss them if they went away. Keeping your senses sharp not only keeps you safe, but it also helps you enjoy life experiences more and remember them later.

TODAY, take some time to focus on each sense individually. Look around you. What do you see that's beautiful? The smile on your spouse's face? The trees? The sky? Appreciate the fact that you can hear the birds and the ocean, as well as oncoming traffic. How does that coffee smell this morning? And the fresh-baked bread you had with lunch, how did that taste? Run your hands through the grass. How does it feel? Prickly? Or soft and lush? Your senses are what make you feel alive. Treat them with respect.

Day 8 Reflections from alcoholexperiment.com

"This lesson reminds me of something my yoga teacher once said: that a body in balance craves what will keep it in balance, whereas a body out of balance will crave what keeps it out of balance. Never thought to apply this to alcohol before. I'm so amazed at how I could convince myself that drinking was no big deal while at the same time knowing that I needed to quit. And now I see how it has contributed to my lifelong low-grade depression, something I thought I was born with and I'd just have to live with. For the first time in my adult life, I'm hopeful that I will finally know what it's like to live with joy. I've been seeing glimpses of that since I quit the sauce, and I like it!"

—PAMELA

"I am learning so much from this experiment. Right now I can't even imagine putting alcohol into my body again. I can see how it has dulled my senses and caused me much grief and anxiety. I find myself looking back at all the things I missed by not being fully present and the mistakes I made due to alcohol. I'm trying not to dwell on the mistakes but use them as a catalyst to move forward."

—FRANCES

"I feel so alive. I was suffering from slight depression but never went to the doctor for any medication. Now I realize the slight depressive feeling I was having every day was the effects of the alcohol. I don't have it anymore, and everything seems sharper and crisper. Coffee smells better, tastes better, and gives me that clean energy in the morning that I could never quite reach after a night of drinking! Also I don't lie awake and worry about my children, money, my health, etc. . . . . Everything that I wanted alcohol to give me, sobriety has given me."

—BILL

▌DAY 9 ▌

The Power of Self-Talk

I AM. Two of the most powerful words;
for what you put after them shapes your reality.
—GARY HENSEL

If you've ever tried to make a change in your life or start a new habit, you know how easily negative thinking and self-talk can defeat your best intentions. You can start the day strong and full of optimism. But as the day wears on, the voice inside your head can get louder and more insistent until it becomes easier to give in. Sometimes it can feel like there's a constant loop of negativity playing in your head, over and over, louder and louder. It's possible you've been experiencing this your whole life in lots of different ways. The good news is that you can change it. The better news is it's not difficult, though it might take some time and practice.

▌ AWARENESS IS KEY

Let's talk about becoming aware of your self-talk. Recognizing what you're telling yourself is the first step. And one way to become deeply aware of how you're talking to yourself is to imagine that the voice inside you that's chattering it up is actually another person. Imagine they're sitting in the chair next to you and just listen objectively. Let them chatter on for a while. Would you ever let a real person talk to you like that? Would you sit and listen to all those negative stories? And would you humor them as they went on and on and on? Of course not. You would never in a million years let somebody sit next to you and never shut up about everything that's wrong with you. Once you personify that voice in your head as an actual individual, you realize how intense and incessant it is. Simply by becoming aware of this self-talk, you have unlocked the door to changing it.

Research shows that most of our thinking is recycled from the day before. In fact, up to 80 percent of your thoughts from today were probably also thoughts you had yesterday. We often give in to what our inner voice is saying simply because it's so repetitious. And repetition masks itself as truth. When something becomes familiar to us, like a thought pattern, we believe it because it's familiar. This is how advertising works. The more often you see an ad on TV or in a magazine, the more likely you are to believe its claims. So whatever you're telling yourself over and over again, eventually you're going to start believing it. Even if it's blatantly not true.

Self-Talk and Cravings

During this experiment, you might be doing a lot of self-talk. I actually want you to recognize two different types. You have the self-talk that is conniving, that will do anything to convince you to pick up a drink. This type of self-talk involves both justifications and comparisons. We'll repeatedly tell ourselves that we need the alcohol, that we won't be okay without it, that we won't be able to sleep without it, and that just one won't hurt. It's also easy to justify our own drinking when we compare our behavior to other people's. If you're a regular drinker, you might say, "Well, at least I'm never fall-down drunk," or "At least I'm not as bad as so-and-so." If you're a binge-drinker, you might say, "Well, at least I don't drink every night." Notice if you're making these kinds of comparisons. Some other self-talk you might be hearing in your head includes things such as:

"This is too hard."

"This has already been too difficult."

"I'm not going to be successful, so I might as well give up now."

All these things are just stories that you tell yourself. And because you repeat them so often, you don't even hear them anymore. You just accept them as true. So you have to stop and hear them again by becoming aware of what you're telling yourself. That way you can make a conscious decision about whether they're actually true. Some people who've been through this process find it helpful to personify the repetitive voice. They call it the Wine Witch or the Alcohol Monster. When you see the voice as something that's not you, it's easier to see through its manipulation.

It's Not Really You

Here's how to recognize that the voice is not really you:

- It tells repetitive stories.
- It has a single aim—to get you to drink.
- It is one-sided and manipulative.

You are stronger than the voice. And it will quickly weaken when you recognize it for what it is and put some distance between you and it. Give it some space. It's very noisy, I get that. But its bark is worse than its bite. It has no actual power over you. It's that little child in the backseat of the car who is desperate for an ice cream. She's not going to give in easily, but ultimately you're in charge.

Self-Talk and Self-Worth

The other type of self-talk, which is possibly more insidious, is the constant negative dialogue we have in our own minds toward ourselves. This is when we beat ourselves up and are harder on ourselves than we would ever be on another human. Here's the thing—you did not create yourself. Think about that for a minute. You are here. You are breathing. But you did not *choose* to be here breathing. You didn't create your beating heart or your hair color or anything else about you. And because of that, you have no right to treat yourself badly. No right. That's the most important thing to realize. Anytime you catch yourself in negative self-talk or beating yourself up, take out a notebook or your phone and write down what you're saying. Write the exact words. Then read them out loud. Would you ever say that to a child or your mother or a good friend? If not, then *stop saying it to yourself!*

You owe it to the universe or God or whoever you believe created you to treat yourself nicely! It's not enough to just repeat a positive mantra a few times a day. When you can talk to yourself like you would talk to your own child or another loved one, you will find that your whole life will shift direction. I'm not talking about now and then. I'm talking about all that repetitive chatter going on in your brain—use words and tones that you would use with that loved one. All the time.

Becoming aware of how you speak to yourself is the first step. The second step is actually changing how you speak to yourself. Most people think this is difficult, because they've been beating themselves up for so long that it's become a habit. And you can't "get rid" of a habit easily, because it's a neurological connection in your brain. It's an unconscious loop that repeats itself over and over. By definition a habit happens without thinking. It's unconscious behavior. Once you wake yourself up and become aware of the habit, you have to make a conscious decision to change it. And to do that, you have to rewire the neurological connections in your brain with new behaviors. It does take effort, but it's completely worth it!

The Power of Gratitude

What helped me get out of the habit of negative self-talk was gratitude. I consciously bring to mind everything I'm grateful for, even the dumbest little things. If I'm writing in my journal, I might notice the pen and think, *I'm thankful that I can write. I'm grateful that I can read and convey my thoughts on paper. Oh look, there's the sky—the clouds are beautiful and I love how they look against the blue. I'm so grateful that I'm alive and I can see and appreciate nature's beauty.* In addition to running through this exercise whenever you become aware of negative self-talk, you can also pick a time every day to stop and think over the past 24 hours and find three to five things you're grateful for.

Here's the kicker: You're probably not going to feel grateful. You'll probably feel cheesy at first. You might think, *I don't feel grateful; I feel angry at myself, which is why I was giving myself such a hard time about my behavior.* It doesn't matter if you feel it. It works anyway. You're suggesting to your subconscious that there's a different pattern it can use, there's a different way to talk to yourself. You're rewiring your brain to look for the positive in everything, and that changes your habit. Trust that you are making changes in your brain, even if you don't feel the results at first. Studies have shown that this simple gratitude exercise can improve your overall happiness in all areas of your life. And I can say that in my experience, that's absolutely true. But it takes practice and patience. So, be nice to yourself, okay?

TODAY, let's do a writing exercise to help you become aware of your negative self-talk. This is adapted for our purposes from Byron Katie's process of questioning our thinking called "The Work" (thework.com). Let's expose your repetitive stories for what they are and diffuse them in your subconscious. Your feelings are preceded by subconscious beliefs. So whenever you start to feel anxious or bad, you can work backward to uncover the belief that's causing the feeling. Once you know the belief, you can use the simple strategy below to help let it go.

Step 1: Identify that you are not feeling your best and use that as a signal to listen to the voice inside your head. What are you thinking right now? What are the thoughts going through your mind? What are the exact words and phrases you used? Write them all down.

Step 2: Ask yourself what are the beliefs or stories underlying these thoughts?

Step 3: Instead of trying to combat the stories or beliefs directly, be sneaky and just ask yourself how they make you feel.

Step 4: Look at the situation and ask yourself how you would feel without those thoughts. Imagine how the moment would feel if you couldn't tell yourself those stories or have those beliefs. What if they just disappeared from your mind? How would you feel? What would be different?

Here's an example:

1. What are you feeling and thinking?

"I'm feeling anxious. My chest is tight and I have a sort of tingling running through me. My muscles are tight. These feelings give me pause, so I back up and listen to my thoughts or self-talk. I might hear, 'I am never going to get ahead at work—I need a beer.' Or 'My kids are out of control. I can't believe I haven't figured out how to get them to behave. Is it five o'clock yet? I can't wait to open that wine bottle I bought this morning.' Or 'Everyone else seems so much happier than I do. What's wrong with me? I'll pour myself this drink, and that will help.'"

2. What stories and beliefs are underlying the thought that I need a drink?

"I believe a drink would make me feel better right now because I think alcohol will help me relax and deal with the stressors in my life."

"I want to numb these uncomfortable feelings, and I know alcohol can do that."

3. How do these stories and beliefs make me feel? Specifically, you might consider how the thought "I need a drink" feels in the context of doing this experiment and the fact you are not drinking right now.

"I feel uncomfortable and upset. I feel deprived. I feel weak when I think I need to have a drink to help me relax. I know that the facts say I won't actually relax. I feel like giving in now will actually make me feel worse."

4. How would you feel without these thoughts? What if you simply couldn't think that you need a drink—how would you be feeling?

It might sound like this: "I'm in a challenging situation, and, yes, there are difficulties, but they aren't compounded by this sense of struggle over drinking."

Or this: "My mind is free to focus on ways to feel better that don't involve alcohol."

There's a huge level of stress and anxiety you're building up here because you're feeling this inner conflict of wanting something you've decided that for now you are not going to have. When you become aware of these conflicting emotions (I want a drink / I'm taking a break from drinking), an amazing thing happens. Your subconscious mind identifies these feelings as painful and naturally lets them go. It's like when you're a toddler and an adult says, "Don't touch that stove. It's hot!" At first you don't know what those words mean, so you have to touch it. You have no reason not to. But once you touch the stove and burn yourself, you're never going to touch it on purpose again. It hurts! That lesson becomes deeply ingrained in your subconscious and you never have to think about not touching a hot stove again. It's the same phenomenon that happens when you simply ask yourself the question, "How do I feel when I believe this story?" When you believe that you need alcohol to relax, but you're not allowing yourself to drink—or when you believe you need alcohol to have a good time, and you're not allowing yourself to drink—how does that feel?

This exercise works because it reveals to your subconscious mind how painful certain stories and beliefs are. Your subconscious says, "Oh, those feelings are painful," and this miraculous thing happens: Your subconscious mind naturally lets go of the belief because it identifies the belief as painful. We aren't always aware of our self-talk, and that is why emotions, even the negative ones, are such a gift. Emotions are the signal that something in our thinking is causing stress. Your job is simply to listen to your thoughts, identify the thoughts causing you stress, and question them. If this works for you and you want to know more about this amazing technique, I highly recommend Byron Katie's book *Loving What Is*.

Day 9 Reflections from alcoholexperiment.com

"I went out with two girlfriends for dinner last night. We all drank water. There was a moment when we were having a great laugh over something and I had the best aha moment mid-laugh! I can absolutely have a great time without booze. I was giddy with happiness over this realization. Slept really well again last night."   —GEORGIA

"Realizing a belief can cause discomfort and that I can change that simply by asking myself honest questions is so empowering. We don't realize how we are programmed by commercialism and advertising. We want to believe that we know what's best for ourselves, but to realize that some of our habits, thoughts, beliefs, or routines aren't actually our own ideas, but rather repetitive messages we take on as fact and live our lives by, is very humbling. Taking back our own thoughts, ideas, and beliefs has helped make me feel whole again."   —RODNEY

"Took a couple of sips of wine with dinner and decided that it wasn't that good, and I got a flash of what my evenings looked like just a couple of weeks ago: too much wine, flushed cheeks, tired, trying not to weave when I get up (don't think I was fooling the hubby), just falling into bed or falling asleep in front of the TV. Zoned out—not connecting. But tonight I threw the wine down the drain after the first couple of sips! Gone. Feels great. I look forward to a good night's sleep and another day tomorrow where I feel rested and relaxed. Also, it's empowering to think about being AF [alcohol-free] during stressful times at work—gives me confidence!"   —MARIA

║║║ ACT #4 ║║║

Alcohol, Our Culture, and Society

▎AWARENESS

We all have an evolutionary need to fit in with a group. It's a survival mechanism. We even have something called mirror neurons in our brains. If we see someone yawn, stretch, or scratch their nose, we're likely to do the same thing. Humans evolved to fit in with others. Think about it. When a prisoner has the harshest punishment inflicted, it's solitary confinement. Being separated from the group is the worst thing we can think of to punish a criminal. Let's name this belief:

"If I don't drink, I won't be part of the group."

So it makes total sense that to fit in with an alcohol-obsessed society, we must be drinkers. But let's break that down so you can decide whether that's something you want to continue.

▎CLARITY

It's pretty easy to figure out where this belief comes from. We all observe evidence of this every single day. Our cultural conditioning practically demands that we drink. We see alcohol all around us, even at church and school functions. Every baby shower, birthday party, wedding, and funeral has some form of alcohol available. All our friends, family members, and authority figures drink. Therefore we should drink, too, just to be considered "normal."

The same attitude used to be true of cigarettes. Do you remember? People smoked because it was just the thing to do. Everyone smoked. Doctors even recommended their favorite brands. That was the reality at one point. Of course, we now know that smoking is dangerous and never should have been encouraged in the first place. And only after many decades of pressure has smoking become "denormalized." Now, smokers are shunned in restaurants, public buildings, and social events. They are forced to go outside to smoke.

Don't think the alcohol industry doesn't know this. It spends billions of dollars each year in the United States alone on advertising to make sure we get the message loud and clear. Cool people drink. Funny people drink. Sexy people drink. And now, thanks to a new trend in alcohol marketing, fit people drink. That's right, the newest trend is to associate drinking with good health. Yoga studios have wine tastings. Low-carb beer brands spend millions on Super Bowl commercials with hard-body athletes. And articles circulate on the internet about how this wine or that spirit can prevent everything from cancer to Alzheimer's disease. So according to the media, if you want to be cool, funny, sexy, and fit, you'd better be a drinker.

We've also experienced that feeling of fitting in when we drink with our friends, right? It's fun. We feel cool, at least for a little while. Whether we're pounding beers at a baseball game or sipping champagne at a classical music festival, it doesn't matter. When our friends are gathered around us, we're all drinking and having a great time. We fit in. The advertising works so well because it mimics our everyday behavior. Or maybe we behave the way we do because the advertising works so well. Either way, order another round—it's halftime! Never mind the consequences in a few hours or the next morning. Never mind the arguments with your spouse or the lost memories or the raging hangover. You've got to be part of the crowd.

So, yes, you probably drink to fit in. And yes, it's a cultural phenomenon. Society's view of nondrinkers is that they're boring. They're buzzkills. They aren't any fun to be around. I find this hilarious now because I'm still the life of the party, even without a drink in my hand. The truth is, the funny people are funny whether they're drinking or not. And the lame people aren't any more interesting just because they're loaded. But the mind is a powerful thing. And since we believe drinkers are more fun, they seem to be. And so we drink, even when we might not want to. And we pressure others to drink, mostly to justify our own choices.

When I wrote *This Naked Mind*, over 7,000 people volunteered to read it and give their feedback. I was shocked to hear that so many of them thought they were alone in their struggle to control their alcohol consumption. They all thought they were the only ones struggling. They thought if they questioned how much they were drinking, people would make fun of them or cast them out of their circle of friends. So they kept the problem hidden, often even from themselves. One of the main reasons people say that they can "take it or leave it" is because they've never tried to leave it.

Once I was honest about my drinking, suddenly others felt like it was okay to question their drinking, too. They worried about the effects on their health and their families but were too afraid to talk about it. In the years since I wrote that book, I've discovered that the people who defend drinking the loudest are often the most worried about how much they drink. They desperately want to have the same amount of fun while drinking less, but they just don't see how it's possible. The cultural conditioning is that strong.

I also want us to ask, What kind of culture are we creating by choosing to be a part of it? It's not popular to talk about, but there is a lot of evidence that an alcohol-saturated culture is actually a culture of violence. According to published studies, in 86 percent of homicide cases, the perpetrator was drinking at the time of the murder. Or what about domestic violence? Fifty-seven percent of the men involved in marital violence were drinking. Seventy-five percent of cases in which a child died from abuse involved alcohol. There's a hotline in the UK that children can call to have a bedtime story read to them if their parents are too drunk to do it. How heartbreaking is that? As a new mother of a baby girl, I'm horrified to hear the alcohol-related statistics for sexual assault. Sixty percent of sexual offenders were drinking at the time of the offense, and sexual assault is at an all-time high. In fact, if you look at the rise in alcohol consumption and the rise in violent crime, they track each other pretty closely. As drinking rates rise, so do the cultural ramifications. Is that the kind of culture we truly want to fit into?

I know it sounds like I want to wipe alcohol off the planet, but that's not the case. What I want is for us, as a culture, to be more mindful of the consequences and think carefully about what we're choosing to promote as normal. Because you're part of this experiment, you have a unique opportunity to be a mindful observer and decide for yourself. Consider whether you can enjoy life and have just as much fun with your friends if you're NOT drinking.

▎ TURNAROUND

The opposite of "*If I don't drink, I won't be part of the group*" is "*If I don't drink, I will still be part of the group*" or "*If I drink, I won't be part of the group.*" Come up with as many ways as you can that the opposites are as true as or truer in your life than the original beliefs.

┃ FITTING IN DURING THE EXPERIMENT

You might be worried that if you stop drinking, you'll lose all your friends, even if it's only for this 30-day experiment. This can be especially challenging if you believe you'll be boring without the alcohol. Since you're not making any immediate decisions about the rest of your life, let's talk about how to get through this experiment while keeping your friendships intact.

1. **Don't preach.** Nobody wants to hear all your research into the dangers of alcohol. They already know most of it, trust me. And at this point, they don't want to be harassed about it. I became an anti-alcohol evangelist at first, and people pitied my husband for having to put up with me. If people ask you about the experiment, give them a brief summary to answer their questions. And maybe point them to this book. Staying low-key will do more good than making them feel like you're judging them. If they want to make a change with their own drinking, they're already judging themselves.

2. **Be a positive example.** Show your friends that you can have just as much fun without drinking (and without talking about it all the time). Let them see for themselves that you simply don't want to drink right now, and that's okay. Again, your friends might feel that by not drinking, you are judging their behavior. Even though this isn't true, they may still think it. So don't isolate them. Be as friendly as ever. Let them know you are doing this for you, and don't try to force the idea on them.

3. **Be creative.** You don't have to tell anyone you're not drinking for 30 days. If you're worried about how your friends will react, don't say anything. It's a personal decision, so keep it to yourself for now. There are lots of ways to explain why you might not

be drinking on a particular evening. Here are some of my favorites from our community:

"I can't tonight; I'm driving."

"I overdid it last night, so I'm taking the night off."

"I'm on a detox that doesn't allow alcohol."

"I'm watching my weight."

"I'm trying to cut back."

"I'm doing an alcohol-free challenge."

"I don't feel like it tonight."

"I have an important meeting tomorrow, so I want to keep a clear head."

If you do decide to continue this 30-day experiment for 60 days, 90 days, or indefinitely, you will eventually want to tell your friends what's going on. And chances are that many of them won't get it. They won't understand. But that doesn't mean they will stop being friends with you. It can take time, but eventually most of them will accept your decision. Keep it all about you, not them. This is a change you've made for yourself. Make sure they know you aren't going to impose your new beliefs on them. Here are some of the phrases I've used:

"I realized I'm happier when I'm not drinking."

"I'm on a health kick, and giving up booze is part of it."

"I decided alcohol was no longer doing me any favors."

"These days I feel better when I don't drink."

"I was no longer having fun with alcohol."

Also be aware that your own attitudes can affect how others in your group treat you. Notice if you're feeling smug or judging your friends for their alcohol consumption. Examine your own treatment of nondrinkers in the past. Do you have some of the same assumptions that you're afraid people will place on you? Also notice the actual reactions you receive from your friends. Your fears may be completely unfounded, after all. Your decision not to drink may be a total nonissue.

Mindful observation is the key to deciding this belief. Can you have as much (or more) fun and fit in with your friends without alcohol? The answer for me is absolutely yes! I'm betting you'll come to the same conclusion. But don't take my word for it. Test it out yourself.

❚ DAY 10 ❚

Dealing with Sugar Cravings

Be gentle with yourself, you're doing the best you can!
—ANONYMOUS

It might surprise you to learn that you may experience heightened sugar cravings during this challenge. This can happen for a couple of reasons. First, most alcoholic drinks contain more than alcohol; in fact, they contain quite a bit of sugar. So your brain is accustomed to the sugar rush from your drink of choice, which will create an intense craving for sugar. Second, both sugar and alcohol create a similar kind of response in the brain.

Let's dig in to why. When the brain perceives something as being important to survival, it produces a chemical called dopamine in response. Dopamine is also called the learning molecule because it is signaled when the brain wants us to repeat the behavior or learn. It is used for reinforcement. A good example of this is the fact that sex is vital for the survival of the species, and so sex produces high levels of dopamine in the brain. Addictive substances cause the brain to flood with dopamine. That is true for alcohol and for sugar, which is also addictive. The dopamine is triggered by the substance, in this case, rather than by something important for survival, but the flood of dopamine tricks the brain into believing that alcohol is vital for survival. Just think—because of the flood of dopamine, your brain is learning that alcohol is important for your very survival. No wonder it's so addictive!

Now, sugar has this same effect. Eating sugar produces huge levels of dopamine. In fact, some studies say that the brain reacts in a similar way to sugar as to substances such as cocaine and heroin. This again is for survival; sugar is incredibly calorie-dense and is an immediate source of energy. If you are trying not to starve, this is a very good thing. However, today it is not necessary and leads to an over-consumption of sugar. When you take a break from alcohol, the loss of a dopamine response causes the brain to seek out the high levels of dopamine in other forms, and sugar is one of the most readily available substitutes. Finally, you may be accustomed to using alcohol as a treat or reward. If you say things like, "I had a hard day and I need a drink" or "I need a drink to relax," you're probably associating alcohol with a treat. But since you're not drinking right now, your brain searches for another way to get that treat or reward, and a very common way to do that is with sugar.

So, you might think you're craving sugar when what you actually want is a treat or reward. Maybe a night out with friends, a movie, or a massage would give you the same feeling of getting a treat, without all the sugar.

At first, I made sure to be gentle with myself. Shaming yourself for any behavior from drinking to eating too much sugar is counterproductive to lasting change and self-acceptance. When I stopped drinking, I knew that I was already accomplishing something amazing by taking a break from booze, and worrying about my sugar intake seemed like a lot to take on at the same time. When I was drinking regularly, I was consuming close to two bottles of wine per day. A bottle of red wine is about 600 to 800 calories, so just by cutting out the drinking, I was saving myself over 1,000 calories. For someone drinking the equivalent amount in beer or mixed drinks, the calorie count is much higher.

I was so happy and proud of myself that I consciously allowed myself to indulge in other areas. I kept gummy bears and fruity candy on hand for those times when I needed an extra boost. I didn't feel the need to eat a lot of baked goods or ice cream, so I bypassed those. Something in the math worked in my favor because I lost 13 pounds in the first 30 days. This is *not* to say that you will have the same experience. You might lose weight; you might not. But you should feel proud of yourself for sticking with the experiment. Indulging in a little extra sugar worked to keep the alcohol cravings at bay and keep me from feeling deprived. This wasn't a long-term strategy or anything (I never carry gummy bears around with me now). It was a way to treat myself gently.

Allowing myself the extra sugar worked for me. However, if you don't want to go that route, here are some ways you can keep the sugar cravings at bay.

1. **Elevate your heart rate.** Exercise naturally boosts serotonin, the happiness hormone. I highly recommend exercising as much as possible during this challenge to help you purge your system of toxins and reduce the cravings naturally. Exercise also reduces stress and lets you get a handle on your emotions in a healthy way without resorting to alcohol to numb away anything you don't want to deal with.

2. **Eat fruit when you feel the need for sugar.** The fiber and fructose (natural sugar) in fruit will keep you satisfied longer than a piece of candy or other processed sweets will.

3. **Drink lots of water.** When you're thinking about sugar, you're often dehydrated and actually craving water. You can add lemon or lime slices and maybe a bit of stevia (a natural sugar substitute) to give a nice flavor to plain water. Your sweet tooth gets satisfied and you're hydrated as well.

4. **Keep your blood sugar stable.** Eating several small meals with

protein throughout the day will stabilize your blood sugar. Protein and fat take longer to digest, which helps keep your energy levels even. In addition, protein breaks down into amino acids, which are responsible for a whole host of processes, including healthy brain function. One amino acid that you need to feel good is GABA (gamma-aminobutyric acid). When you feel low, it's often because you don't have enough protein in your system to produce amino acids. Alcohol produces GABA in excess. So when you take the alcohol away, you're going to need to replace that amino acid at healthy levels. Eating enough protein will do the job. I have noticed a direct correlation between how much protein I eat and my anxiety levels throughout the day. Eventually, I was able to wean myself off my depression medication, which was great. But eating protein was also a key component to keeping my moods and energy levels stable.

5. **Consume naturally fermented food and drinks.** Wait, fermented? Aren't we trying to get away from fermented drinks? Yes, we are, but these contain such a tiny level of alcohol that they shouldn't cause a problem. And there are so many health benefits to fermented foods. Foods like sauerkraut, kimchi, kefir, and kombucha are fermented naturally and contain live cultures (probiotics). Studies have shown that eating fermented foods is one of the best ways to reduce cravings for sugar and processed foods. Be aware that cooking kills off the good stuff. So canned sauerkraut or processed and sugar-laden yogurt isn't going to work. You need to buy naturally fermented foods that require refrigeration to keep the cultures alive.

▌BABY STEPS

There's definitely a temptation to do everything at once. You might be thinking, *Oh, well, I'm taking a break from alcohol, so I might as well quit sugar, start meditating, and run five miles every day. I'm going to be the best version of me!* While that's a noble thought, it rarely works in the long term. Once you start down the path to self-improvement, it's natural to want to pile on the good habits and become a brand-new person. But studies show that this is a recipe for failure. Take baby steps and be gentle with yourself. Focus on this one goal of eliminating alcohol for 30 days, and then you can revisit your other goals next month. Because the beautiful thing is that once you tackle this cornerstone habit and reduce or eliminate your alcohol intake, you'll begin to implement a whole host of other habits almost by default. I'm a different person. I exercise regularly, including my weekly tae kwon do practice and my daily mindfulness practice. And I started a business. All these changes stemmed from changing my drinking. I didn't know it at the time, but making that big change caused a positive ripple effect across so many aspects of my life.

TODAY, make a plan for how you're going to tackle sugar cravings whenever they come up. If you're going to let yourself indulge in sugary foods during the experiment, what choices will you make? Do you have them in your pantry at the moment? If not, you might want to consider stocking up. If you plan to exercise, what will you do exactly? How can you prevent those cravings from showing up in the first place?

Day 10 Reflections from alcoholexperiment.com

"I know I'm one of those people who can overdo it with the self-improvement tasks, so I'm trying to be okay with an imperfect diet that includes some comfort foods while I get through the first 30 days of not drinking and get used to being someone who doesn't drink. Quitting alcohol is hard enough. I'm choosing to be okay with pasta and dessert for now as long as I'm also eating more nutrient-dense foods, too."   —LEIGH

"I have found that cutting out drinking has given me more time and energy to put in place healthy habits that have only been thoughts before. I'm being careful to start out slow but consistent. I'm not craving sugar so much as that 'treat,' which has been a bit of a struggle to satisfy. I find that my appetite has increased, so I've started eating smaller meals more often. Also, I'm craving carbs more! Does that have something to do with alcohol? I would expect so. Just being mindful about that, too. And yes, *gentle* is the word for this experiment . . . in every way!"   —ROSS

The Alcohol Culture Is Shifting

Don't be afraid of being different.
Be afraid of being the same as everyone else.
—ANONYMOUS

Drinking has become so prevalent, so pervasive in our culture, that it's difficult to escape its influence. But there's an amazingly vibrant minority of people who are taking a step back and thinking about that status quo. They've found they are participating in something that isn't much fun anymore, and they're choosing to pause and reflect. The result is an entire culture shift around alcohol.

I first noticed the shift in some of the super-athletes and people who are deeply involved in the fitness and health world. They realized that while they were eating all-organic food, exercising, and doing yoga, they were also drinking a known toxin in excessive amounts. People are waking up, and they're starting to question that behavior.

❚ YOUNG PEOPLE ARE DRINKING LESS

The idea that drinking alcohol might not be such a great idea is becoming more prevalent among young people as well. Young people today are drinking much less than their counterparts were 10 years ago. This change is motivated in part by a desire for better health and to buck their parents' drinking trend. I've heard people say that alcohol is their "parents' drug," and so these young people are choosing not to drink. According to a recent poll, 66 percent of adults under 24 years old in America don't feel that alcohol is important to their life.

If you contrast that with older people, the opposite is true. Drinking among older generations, especially women, is going up. In fact, according to a recent study, there was a whopping 107 percent increase in alcohol use disorder (AUD) among adults 65 and over, and an 82 percent increase in AUD among those 45 to 65 years old.[1] So, a very intelligent, mindful minority believe that alcohol is less important to their social life than it was to their parents'. In fact, the study says that 41 percent of Gen Y drinkers think alcohol is less important to their own life than it was to their parents' lives. I believe social media has contributed to this new attitude, too. When your entire life is documented on Instagram and Snapchat, you don't want to be caught drunk or passed out. Seeing videos of their friends' behavior can also be a deterrent.

CUTTING BACK IS A GLOBAL PHENOMENON

Drinking less is not only a local phenomenon; it's global. In the UK, a fifth of British adults under 25 don't drink at all. And that number has been drastically increasing, according to the UK's Office for National Statistics. According to the National Drug Strategy Household Survey in Australia, the percentage of teenagers drinking there was cut in half in 2016. And weekly risky drinking among 18- to 24-year-olds dropped from 32 to 22 percent between 2010 and 2013. The declines are happening across the board—in both sexes and in all sorts of socioeconomic strata, and in both urban and rural areas. Similar studies have come out in Canada and Sweden.

A UK program called Dry January, in which people stop drinking alcohol for the month, has expanded globally over the years. In 2017, 5 million people signed up to do Dry January. According to research by the Public Health England, 67 percent of people will cut back their drinking over the rest of the year after participating in Dry January. And 8 percent of those people will stop drinking completely because they feel so good.

Other exciting things show evidence of this trend toward less alcohol consumption. The first alcohol-free bars are opening in major cities like London and New York City. The first nonalcoholic spirit, called Seedlip, has come out. And there's an alcohol-free rave movement called Daybreaker, in which people gather to watch the sun rise and have a massive dance party.

You might be surprised to learn that some of the most successful entrepreneurs, musicians, authors, and actors don't drink. This list includes Warren Buffett, Tony Robbins, Tobey Maguire, Stephen King, Daniel Radcliffe, Tyra Banks, Natalie Portman, Jada Pinkett Smith, Bradley Cooper, Larry Ellison, Christina Ricci, Bruce Willis, Eric Clapton, Jim Carrey, David Beckham, Jennifer Lopez, Ben Affleck, Eminem, David Murdock, Tim McGraw, Keith Urban, Joe Manganiello, and Gerard Butler.

There's also a culture of start-up entrepreneurs who are no longer drinking. Entrepreneurship comes with intense amounts of stress, as men and women work themselves around the clock to achieve success. Many extremely successful entrepreneurs have identified alcohol abstinence as their keystone habit. It's the one thing that allows everything else to fall into place. Suddenly it's cool to be a nondrinker.

You're in good company when you choose to take a break from alcohol. You're actually part of an amazing, vibrant, and healthy culture shift.

TODAY, keep your eyes open and see if you can catch people not drinking. Notice how many people are choosing iced tea, water, or soda over alcohol. And realize you're not alone.

Day 11 Reflections from alcoholexperiment.com

"I'm so incredibly grateful for the Alcohol Experiment. I can't imagine going back. Looking back at the moments lost and mistakes made is incredibly hard but hugely rewarding. Even though I considered myself a functioning drinker, I don't think I was really fooling anyone. I'm sure I have said and done things that have hurt those around me over the years. It's a hard pill to swallow, but I will use it as a building block of my new sober life. I feel as if I've experienced a rebirth of sorts. I will forgive myself and move forward."   —PATRICK

"I have been plagued with depression for years, which only got worse with alcohol when sober and the false reality that I could only be happy when drinking. I have been asking myself where have I gone? I've felt lost and detached from myself. I've lost my interests, passions, and drive. Like Annie said, children are the happiest people and they don't drink. I would often reflect back to myself as a child and wonder where I had gone. Now that I understand alcohol was contributing to this, I am experiencing all these emotions again and loving life for the first time in a long time."   —MILLIE

||| ACT #5 |||

Alcohol and Happiness

| AWARENESS

For so many of us, alcohol has been central to so many meaningful and fun events in our lives that we blend the two together without thinking. Holidays, birthdays, weddings—celebrations of all kinds practically require alcohol in some form or another. So it's no wonder we feel like alcohol makes us happy. It seems like it's always there when we're having fun. Let's name this belief:

> "Alcohol makes me happy."

| CLARITY

Where did this belief come from? We've been conditioned to believe that drinking makes us happy. We see people on TV, in movies, and all around us smiling and laughing while drinking. How can we help but smile as the gang shouts, "Norm!" or Carrie Bradshaw polishes off another cosmo with her best friends?

We've also experienced this belief in our own lives. When we drink, we think we feel happier because our filters are removed. Isn't it interesting that every time we've been in a fun social setting there was alcohol involved? These experiences cemented your belief, and alcohol became deeply intertwined with happiness. We feel free to express ourselves without boundaries. We think we're funnier and the life of the party, at least for a little while.

So is it true? Does alcohol really make you happy?

Let's start by defining what *happiness* means to you. Does it mean something fleeting and temporary, like a fun evening out? Or is it something more? Take some time to think about this. Write down some situations that describe happiness for you. Then ask yourself, Did you always need alcohol to be happy? When you were a kid, did you need a six-pack before every Little League game? Or did you and your girlfriends play hopscotch with real scotch? The average four-year-old laughs hundreds of times a day, no alcohol required. Think back and recall the years before you started drinking. Remember those friendships and activities that brought you joy.

Okay, now let's talk about how much time you actually spend drinking. I know for me, I would get off work around 6:00 p.m. and I'd probably drink until 10:00 or 11:00. Then I'd go to bed. I can remember feeling relieved for the first half hour of the evening, happy that my stressful day was over. But I don't remember feeling overly happy and joyous for the other four hours. I do remember waking up around 3:00 every morning and fretting for at least an hour over what I'd done—worrying about what I might have said or what I might not remember the next day. I remember dreading the morning hangover. Can I say that the few hours of drinking offered enough happiness to overcome the dread and keep me going for the whole next day? No, I can't. For me, it wasn't worth it.

The pursuit of happiness is so ingrained into human existence that no matter how happy we are, we're constantly on the hunt for more. When we see others laughing and enjoying themselves, we naturally want what they have. If they have a beer in their hand, we want one, too. If they're drinking champagne toasts at midnight, we want to do it, too. Whether it's a party, a sporting event, or a concert, did the alcohol actually cause the fun? Or were you in a happy environment and the alcohol wasn't actually the key component?

Happiness is at the very heart of advertising, especially alcohol advertising. But there's no balance in advertising. Alcohol actually causes far more unhappiness than happiness. It slows our minds and chemically depresses us. The ads never show the unhappiness that alcohol causes.

You don't see the middle-of-the-night anxiety or tears because we've again broken our promises to ourselves.

You don't see the drunken fights where people who love each other are now screaming at each other like they are mortal enemies.

You don't see the morning-after neglect that children suffer because their parents have painful hangovers and can't get out of bed.

You don't see the emotional, physical, and sexual abuse.

You don't see the drunk driver's face after they cause a fatal accident.

You don't see the husband taking his own life because he's lost everything—his family, his job, his money, his home, his self-respect.

You don't see the arguments and fistfights.

You don't see the violent crimes.

You don't see the unwanted pregnancies.

In short, you don't see the sheer and unrelenting misery that alcohol can cause.

Drinking doesn't just make the drinker unhappy. It makes the people around them unhappy, too. How many times does a spouse have to put up with their partner coming home drunk and starting a fight before they decide to leave? How many jobs does a drinker have to go through before they lose their family's home? How long will a girlfriend put up with mediocre sex and frequent hangovers before she decides she can do better? The damage alcohol does in our society is so widespread; we all have a story about alcohol and how it has destroyed someone we know.

And the children. Alcohol's effect on children is heartbreaking. Their whole world revolves around their parents. Their minds, bodies, and beliefs are tied to their parents' behavior. They model what they see and hear. Do they hear people at the bar laughing at their mom's jokes? Or do they hear her sharp tone with them when she gets home, the alcohol is wearing off, and her anger is flaring? Do they see groups of friends enjoying an evening concert? Or do they only see the hangover in the morning? What about when it gets really bad? Leading to emotional or even physical abuse? And children of alcoholics are up to four times more likely to develop alcohol addiction later in life.[1] It's a terrible cycle all based on the false belief that drinking makes us happy.

But maybe you think I'm being extreme here. Maybe you've never gone to such extremes, and that postwork drink is a harmless habit that seems to make you happy. But here's the question: Does it actually make you happier overall? It's true, there's a bit of a rush when alcohol first enters your system. Alcohol is an interesting substance because it is both a stimulant and a depressant. Alcohol acts as a temporary stimulant just after it enters your system while your blood alcohol content (BAC) is rising. A rising BAC affects the parts of the brain responsible for elation and excitement. But after only 20 to 30 minutes, your BAC starts to fall and the depressive effects take over, and people report feeling uneasy, sad, lonely, restless, and generally unhappy.

Since the rush doesn't last, and you end up feeling worse than you did before that first drink because of a falling BAC, you need another hit to keep the BAC rising. But that initial nice tipsy feeling never comes back in quite the same way, no matter how many drinks you consume. You drink more and more to get that rush back. But the more alcohol you consume, the duller your senses become. Your perceptions change and you can no longer assess how drunk you are. It's possible to keep the BAC rising for four hours or so. But once your BAC crosses a certain threshold (0.05 or 0.06), the alcohol becomes a downer, even if your BAC continues to rise. What's more is that the longer you keep drinking, the longer it's going to take for your BAC to come back down. And that means 10 or more *hours* of feeling uneasy, anxious, upset, and even depressed. How fun is that?

Look at it logically. If a little alcohol makes you happy, shouldn't a lot of alcohol make you happier? So how come the more you drink, the less you feel that euphoria? The more you drink, the more likely you'll do or say something embarrassing. The more you drink, the more likely you'll feel terrible in the morning. How can that possibly be defined as happiness?

But we all see friends and families giggling, joking, and enjoying themselves while drinking. Have you ever stopped to consider that maybe they'd be enjoying themselves as much (if not more) without the drinks? Maybe it's the occasion and not the alcohol providing the happiness. It's hard to separate the occasion from the drink, though, because drinking is completely intertwined with every social event we attend.

Yet, when I look back now, it's almost a joke how much happier I am without drinking! I can finally truly enjoy social occasions for what they are—a chance to hang out with my friends and have a good time. Whether they're drinking or not doesn't affect my own enjoyment. Only after alcohol has completely left your system can you fully realize that, yes, you can feel joy and happiness and incredible energy levels on a consistent basis.

When Does the Fun Begin?

Let's consider this from a different angle. Think back to the last good time you had fun drinking. Maybe it was last night. Maybe it was a few hours ago. Think about when, exactly, the fun began. At what point did you start to feel good about the experience? Because I usually drank after work, my fun began the minute I'd walk out of my office. It was like I could finally breathe. The workday was done. I could relax. I'd already be feeling good just anticipating spending the next few hours doing something fun. I'd reach for my first glass of wine with a smile on my face. For me, these feelings began 15 to 20 minutes or so before I even took my first sip. The anticipation of having the rest of the evening in front of me made me feel good.

The same thing happens with the Friday effect. It's Friday night.

You've got the whole weekend ahead of you, and you're feeling good. Naturally, you celebrate with a few beers down at the pub with your mates. Ordering that first round gets you into the weekend mood, right? But the cheering and excitement and fun happen well before any alcohol has had time to take effect in your body. You don't even have the drink in front of you yet.

So ask yourself, "When does the fun actually begin?" Is it when you're drinking? Or is it the anticipation beforehand that kicks things off? Could the fun actually be coming from the connection you have to the people and places you frequent when you drink? Also ask yourself, "How do I define *fun*?" What does that mean for you, and how does alcohol make things fun? How does it make you happy?

True connection and pleasure come from consciously experiencing a moment in time. You have to be present and aware of what's happening around you for it to register as happiness in your brain. But alcohol's chemical effect on your mind is the exact opposite of being present and aware. Alcohol numbs your physical and emotional experience. It makes you less and less aware as the night goes on until you can't even remember what happened the next morning.

TURNAROUND

The opposite of *"alcohol makes me happy"* is *"alcohol makes me sad"* or *"alcohol doesn't make me happy."* Come up with as many ways as you can that the opposite is as true as or truer in your life than the original belief.

Try the Happiness Exercise

The world's leading happiness researcher, Barbara Fredrickson, says the 10 most positive emotions that combine to create the emotion we call happiness are joy, gratitude, serenity, interest, hope, pride, amusement, inspiration, awe, and love. I want you to take the time to do this short happiness exercise because it will completely shift your subconscious feelings about alcohol in a truly profound way. Please write your answers down on paper, because writing cements your thoughts to your subconscious.

Consider each of these emotions, one at a time. Take the first one, joy. Write down all the ways alcohol increases joy in your life. Take as much time as you need. Then write down all the ways alcohol robs you of joy in your life. Think about your reality now—not what life used to be like or what you hope it will be in the future. Right now. How does alcohol add joy? How does it take joy away? Then go on to gratitude. Ask yourself the same questions. And follow that with the next emotion, continuing until you've covered all 10: joy, gratitude, serenity, interest, hope, pride, amusement, inspiration, awe, and love.

This exercise will give you an incredible perspective on how much joy you're truly receiving from alcohol, and how much you're losing. Research has shown that only 10 percent of our overall happiness depends on external things, whether that's a new car, a relationship, or alcohol. Things don't make us happy. Ninety percent depends on our internal environment. How relaxed are we? How confident? How peaceful? You have the power to make changes that will truly make you happy. And that's great news, because while we can't always change our outer environment, we can absolutely influence what's going on internally.

Your Incredible Body and Brain

Take care of your incredible body. It is the most amazing thing
you own, and it is the only place you truly have to live.
—ANONYMOUS

Today I want to take a minute to celebrate the incredible miracle that
is you! Most of us don't take the time to think about how amazing our
bodies and our brains are. Think about all the incredible physical and
mental feats we can perform. Our brains are more powerful than
supercomputers; in fact, we created supercomputers. We've developed
cures for diseases. We've even propelled ourselves off this planet and
onto the moon. Is there anything we can't do if we put our minds to
it? Our minds are powerful, and since we don't fully understand their
power, they can sometimes work against us.

We've already discussed your mind's incredible ability to hinder
your growth and progress. But it's so important to understand, that I
want to go into more detail here. Neuropsychologists have shown that
we actually create what we anticipate. When we anticipate something
negative, it becomes reality. And so, for example, if you anticipate that
giving up drinking is going to be difficult, that you're going to be deprived and not have any fun, then that becomes your reality. Some
people call this the placebo effect, and it's absolutely real. There was
an interesting study done in which people were exposed to poison ivy.
Doctors rubbed poison ivy on one arm of each participant and told

them that it was actually a plain leaf. Then they rubbed a plain leaf on each participant's other arm and told them that it was poison ivy. All but two people experienced an allergic reaction to the plain leaf and did not react at all to the actual poison ivy.

If somebody brushes up against poison ivy in nature, they will have a reaction. There is a physical reaction that happens when those chemical compounds come in contact with the skin—you get an itchy rash. Yet if your brain *believes* that nothing should happen, then nothing happens.

If your brain is strong enough to overcome a reaction to exposure to the chemical compound in poison ivy, it's also strong enough to ensure you are miserable at a party if you've decided you will be miserable without drinking.

I THE HEALING PHARMACY WITHIN

Your brain and body's function is to ensure you survive and thrive. Consider that for a moment. This amazing living computer is not meant to ingest large amounts of alcohol every single day. If it were, it would have been built into our physiology. Instead, we have an infinite, incredible pharmacy within us. We deliver all the right emotions and chemicals that we need to live a healthy and balanced life, in the right doses, at the right times. Consider the fight-or-flight response. If you're being attacked by a bear in the wilderness, your body responds to help you escape that bear. Your heart starts beating faster, you become lighter on your feet. Parents have been able to pick up very heavy objects that have landed on their children because our bodies can release chemicals that make us 10, 20, even 30 times stronger than normal if we need to be in an extreme moment.

Our bodies and our brains can do such incredible stuff, and so often we overlook it. We don't even consider how intricate and powerful we are. There's a lot of talk these days about loving ourselves, and certainly we need to love ourselves. But we confuse loving ourselves with thinking that we're beautiful, sexy, talented, or good at all these external things. In my opinion, that is not truly loving ourselves.

When you have a child, you love that child not because of their behavior, but simply because they exist. You want to feed that child good food and take care of their body because you want them to be healthy. We need to love ourselves as we love our children. Loving yourself includes getting to know yourself, accepting yourself, and making a conscious decision not to take your health for granted. You are the person you will be spending the most time with for the rest of your life, so stop judging yourself and take a minute to appreciate the true, miraculous nature of this body and mind that you've been given. We need to care for ourselves out of love and compassion, remembering that we were created whole, complete with everything we need to not only survive but thrive. We must take care of our bodies to accomplish what we set out to do in the world. We love our bodies out of gratitude, because they keep us alive and healthy, and because they house our personalities—the very essence of who we are.

Some of the most impressive people in the world don't drink. Not because they've had a problem with it, but simply because they naturally don't want to put alcohol into their bodies. Comedic actor Jim Carrey once said, "I'm very serious about no alcohol, no drugs. Life is too beautiful."

TODAY, take some time to appreciate how amazing your body is. Give it a great big *thank-you* for keeping you alive.

Day 12 Reflections from alcoholexperiment.com

"I have never really considered how lucky I am to have the body I do. I should really be filled with joy and gratitude for the 48 years my body has gotten me through . . . with very few complaints. I've never thanked it, appreciated it, given it unconditional love. And yet it keeps doing its best for me every minute. A thankless, never-ending job that hasn't been easy. . . . The booze, cigarettes, lack of sleep, physical exertion, stress, etc., over the years . . . and yet the body comes out swinging every day to do its best for me. I have completely taken my body for granted. I've only pummeled it and criticized it my whole life. That is just so sad. I treat my body worse that I would ever treat someone I hate. Let me be grateful for this body I've been given and appreciate it every day by being conscious of how I treat it and what I put in it."
—PRISCILLA

"I'm just starting to get a glimpse of how wondrous and unlimited life could be if I wasn't groveling around in the mud every day with alcohol and hangovers. And that, then, leads me to realize how much precious time—and life—I've wasted in the last 35 years."
—JONATHAN

||| ACT #6 |||

Is Alcohol Healthy in Moderation?

| AWARENESS

We all know that drinking too much is bad for us. You know, in a very general, fuzzy sort of way. But science! We've all seen so many reports and studies that prove it's healthy for us in moderation, right? Beer lowers our risk for heart disease, right? Red wine is good for my heart, and it also has the ability to improve cholesterol, fight free-radical damage, help manage diabetes, fight obesity, and prevent cognitive decline. Doesn't it?

Let's name this belief:

"Alcohol is healthy in moderation."

Yeah, let's dig into this one.

| CLARITY

It makes total sense that you believe alcohol is good for your health when you take into account the hundreds of articles you've probably seen promoting this research. It's no accident that many drinkers can quote scientific studies and comparative mortality rates between drinkers and nondrinkers.

It's easy to convince yourself that there may be some truth to these articles because you haven't experienced the opposite and because it makes us feel better about our choices. After all, if you've never had a heart attack or stroke, who's to say the three bottles of wine you drink every night aren't contributing to that? You don't have Alzheimer's. So it's possible your alcohol consumption has something to do with that. Antioxidants are good for us. So the wine you drink with antioxidants must be good for you, too. Our brains are excellent at rationalizing. And the alcohol industry counts on that when they promote this kind of pseudoscientific reporting.

The fact is, there are a handful of studies claiming that alcohol is good for you. Some of them were even funded by the alcohol industry itself. And there are thousands of studies that prove the exact opposite. The difference is that the positive studies get far more attention than the negative ones. Why do you suppose that is?

First of all, people share information based on something called social currency. If I think an article will raise people's opinion of me, then I'll share it. If the post makes me look funny, smart, or righteously outraged, I'm much more likely to send it along to all my friends. Our friends hang around us because we all think and believe more or less the same things. So if I drink, and I believe it's healthy, there's a good chance my friends do, too. And we all want our beliefs confirmed by science. So I may share an article about alcohol lowering cholesterol so that all of us can feel better about our drinking habits.

Secondly, there's a marketing concept that familiarity breeds belief. The more often you hear or see something, the more likely you are to believe it. (Which explains a lot of what goes on in politics.) So every time you see a health benefit touted in a social media post or blog article, it reinforces your belief that alcohol is healthy in moderation.

Economics come into play here, too. Journalists make money by writing popular articles that get attention. They live and die by their likes, clicks, and engagement. The more readers who see an article, the more advertising is sold, and the more value those journalists bring to their news or online organization. Telling people that drinking is healthy gets clicks. And these days it doesn't seem to matter if the information is taken out of context or even completely fabricated.

We believe alcohol is healthy in moderation because our friends tell us, the media tells us, and scientific studies tell us it's true. We've heard it so many times it's become "common knowledge."

So, is drinking really healthy for us? Since thousands upon thousands of studies typically aren't reported on, let's look at the most obvious evidence we can find. How about vomiting? That's normal, right? If we drink too much, we throw up. If you think about the mechanics of vomit, it's actually pretty miraculous. Our bodies have an automatic rejection reflex if we ingest anything that's harmful to us. We don't die, because our bodies know better. Unfortunately, alcohol is an anesthetic and numbs our gag reflex, which means we don't vomit as soon as we should, given how much we've consumed. So the poison takes effect and we get hangovers.

Sometimes we even come to believe that worshiping the porcelain throne is a badge of honor. Look at me! I'm working today even though I'm super-hungover. I'm so tough. Give me a prize. The internal evidence is staring you right in the face as it pours out of you in rivers. And it's gross! How can something your body reacts to so negatively be good for you?

Let's also look more closely at the popularly cited evidence to support the idea that alcohol is good for us. We've all heard about the health benefits of resveratrol and antioxidants in wine. There are ways to get those same antioxidants without addictive and life-destroying effects, but let's say for the sake of argument that we think the research shows alcohol is good for our hearts. Diving in more deeply, there's more evidence that shows the opposite. There are scientists who study scientific studies. They pull together all the data on the participants and they analyze the findings until they come up with their own conclusions. A study published in the *British Medical Journal* looked at this idea that alcohol is heart-healthy.[1] It analyzed the drinking habits and cardiovascular health of over a quarter of a million people and concluded "that a reduction in alcohol consumption, even for light to moderate drinkers, is beneficial for cardiovascular health." Huh.

But wait—don't drinkers live longer than nondrinkers? One wildly popular study, the Holahan study,[2] has been widely publicized in mainstream news outlets like CBS News,[3] *Time*,[4] and even *Medical News Today*.[5] Its creator, Charles J. Holahan, claims that people who drink live longer than abstainers. I think it's worth taking the time to analyze this study a bit so you can see where this social belief comes from.

The study took 1,824 people ages 55 to 65 and then looked at how many were alive 20 years later. Of them, 1,479 were drinkers and 345 were not. They found that a higher percentage of nondrinkers had died during the period of the study. So, they found a correlation between drinking and death. Correlation is not causation. They did not measure or account for the cause of death at all, so we have no idea how these people died. If you look more deeply into the study, you'll find that they say the abstainers were more likely to have had prior problems with alcohol, which is why they didn't drink. Interesting. It also goes on to say that they were more likely to be obese and smoke cigarettes.

Come on! We're saying that drinkers live longer based on a study of only 345 people who had prior alcohol problems *and* were obese smokers? Really? Think about that for a second. Are you willing to risk your health based on such a small, skewed sample?

According to the World Health Organization, "alcohol can damage nearly every organ and system in the body. Its use contributes to more than 60 diseases and conditions."[6] The WHO also reports that alcohol has surpassed AIDS as the leading risk factor for death among males between the ages of 15 and 59.[7] And a groundbreaking and incredibly comprehensive global study came out in 2018 stating that there is in fact no safe level of drinking; even a single drink, even on occasion, is detrimental to your health.[8]

In a study of the harmful effects of 20 different drugs, alcohol came in as the most dangerous drug.[9] It's more harmful than heroin or crack cocaine when you look at the "ratio between toxicological threshold [or how much it will take to kill you] and estimated human intake."[10]

The International Agency for Research on Cancer declared alcohol a carcinogen in 1988. Not only is alcohol pure ethanol, which is extremely toxic, but it can contain at least 15 other carcinogenic compounds, including arsenic, formaldehyde, and lead.

We've also known alcohol causes cancer for 30 years, and yet it's news to most drinkers. No matter how little or what type of alcohol you're drinking, you're increasing your risk of cancer of the breast, mouth, throat, rectum, liver, esophagus, and other organs. Cancer Research UK says, "There is no safe limit for alcohol when it comes to cancer." Why don't we know this? People just don't talk about such things.

The term "drink responsibly" came from the alcohol industry itself. It wants you to feel good about your drinking, think that you're being socially responsible. Never mind that you're probably killing yourself. I know this is depressing. It should make you angry. But the good news is that any reduction in alcohol consumption lowers your risk for cancer. The fact that you're reading this book and taking a break is helping your body heal itself.

It's incredible to me that in our society more attention is given to the side effects of even the most benign prescription drugs, which must all be listed individually in the advertisement, yet there is no disclaimer in alcohol ads. Fortunately, you can decide for yourself. Now that you know some of the risks and the ways that science gets reported, take some time to think about what you're truly doing to yourself. Is it worth the risk?

| TURNAROUND

The opposite of "*alcohol is healthy in moderation*" is "*alcohol is not healthy in moderation.*" Come up with as many ways as you can that the opposite is as true as or truer in your life than the original belief.

| DAY 13 |

Let's Talk About Sex

"All my senses are awakened. Sex is more fantastic than ever!"
—CARRIE (ALCOHOL EXPERIMENT PARTICIPANT)

Yes, I am going there. Why? Because this was a major barrier for me. I was convinced that I needed a few glasses of wine to "get in the mood," and I was terrified of sober sex. I'll tell you all about my personal experience, but first let's have a look at what the science says.

▌ SAFE SEX

Let's get safe sex out of the way before we dig into the juicier stuff. The truth is that sex is not much fun if it results in unwanted pregnancy or STDs. Studies show that women are more likely to sleep with someone they don't feel comfortable with and less likely to use a condom after they've been drinking. And men are more likely to misinterpret a woman's interest, which can lead to all sorts of unwanted situations and consequences.

Alcohol, Testosterone, and Libido

Drinking reduces testosterone levels in both men[1] and women. We've probably all heard of (or been in) situations where a man can't perform because he drank too much. This is why. In one study done on rats, their testicles decreased by 50 percent when they were fed a steady diet of ethanol. And yes, ethanol is the same thing that is in both your gas tank and that bottle of tequila. A reduction in testosterone for men means some pretty unpleasant side effects, like shrinking testicles, breast enlargement, fatigue, lowered libido, decreased sperm production, and, of course, erectile dysfunction.

In women, low testosterone can be responsible for some pretty unsexy side effects, including hair loss, weight gain, fatigue, disrupted sleep, depression, and anxiety. But that's not the worst of it. Reduced testosterone in women is also responsible for decreased libido and a condition called anorgasmia, which is the *inability to have orgasms!* Now that's no fun!

Reduced testosterone is not the only way that alcohol affects libido. As the amount of alcohol in the body increases, the brain's ability is impaired and less able to sense sexual stimulation. Further, as a depressant, alcohol affects libido by interfering with the parts of the nervous system that are essential for arousal and orgasm, including circulation, respiration, and the sensitivity of nerve endings. According to the Mayo Clinic, alcohol is a common cause of erectile dysfunction. This is for two reasons. First, dehydration can lead to an increase in the hormone that is associated with erectile dysfunction: angiotensin. Dehydration also causes a decrease in blood volume, which makes it more difficult to both get and maintain an erection. Alcohol also causes circulatory issues, which means that no matter how much a man wants sex, alcohol can make it physically impossible to sustain, or even get, an erection.[2]

The bottom line, no matter whether you are a man or a woman, is that while alcohol may lessen your inhibitions to fall into bed, it will decrease your ability to become and stay aroused. Not to mention your enjoyment. Which leads me to . . .

Sober Sex Is Truly Better Sex

Yes, I know you might find that hard to believe. I surveyed hundreds of people who have taken part in the Alcohol Experiment, and the truth is . . . sober sex is better sex! Your brain is receiving the full impact and unimpeded information from your senses—and wow. I had no idea sex could feel that good. When I was drinking, I rarely remembered it the next day, and I certainly don't remember having the level of pure physical enjoyment that sex now brings. And all the science backs this up! You are literally more in touch with your body when you aren't drinking and more present to the experience. The signals your nerves send are stronger without alcohol—meaning not only are orgasms stronger, but also it is easier to have one (or many)!

But you don't have to take my word for it. Here are some recent posts in the Alcohol Experiment community about sober sex:

"My second day AF I had the best sex of my life. I've been sold on being AF from that point on."   —Tracy

"Sober sex is the best! It had been so long since I'd had sex sober that I forgot how much I really enjoyed it."   —Kelly

"Completely agree on sober sex being better. So much easier and quicker to umm . . . you know . . . I'll just say it, orgasm! LOL. Finally feel like sex doesn't have to be a chore with the husband, but actually look forward to it now."   —Kim

"Right!? Sober sex is one of my main motivations for staying sober. Things in the bedroom have gotten fun again."   —Lori

And the best part? You get to find all this out for yourself!

| HOW TO GET IN THE MOOD

Yet it's true that alcohol does lower our inhibitions. While this leads to all sorts of unpleasant things—like sleeping with someone you just met, or don't really like—it can also be difficult to get in the mood if you aren't used to sex without drinking. Here are a few things you can do to get in the mood.

It may sound obvious, but wait until you get to know someone enough that you trust them enough to want to have sex. This is another huge benefit of sober sex; the people we have sex with are actually people we like and want to have sex with!

Sexy massage is an amazing way to calm your nerves and get in the mood. It awakens all the senses, sends relaxing signals throughout the body and brain, and allows you to get into the moment and the mood. Not to get too personal, but I recommend warm oil and candlelight.

Communicate. Again, this may be a no-brainer, but it's amazing how little we actually communicate during sex. Let your partner know what you want and what you like. Talk through any anxieties you have. Open, honest communication is truly sexy.

Don't wait to be in the mood. This is one of the biggest barriers to sober sex. Women especially often get in the mood after they are being touched, after that nice massage, during a couple's bath. If you wait until you're in the mood, not only will you create more fear around sober sex, but you will also reinforce your beliefs that alcohol is vital to sex. The truth is that nothing can influence our subconscious mind like our own experiences, and by showing up and giving yourself the experience of sober sex, you can easily (and enjoyably!) prove to yourself that everything I am saying is true.

The great thing is that by doing it a few times your body will remember what it is made for, and, like everything else, you will decouple the belief that alcohol is necessary for sex. Realizing you don't need alcohol to have sex can be a major aphrodisiac.

Day 13 Reflections from alcoholexperiment.com

"The sex thing was a huge issue for me. I'd spent most of my life using alcohol to get in the mood. I avoided it as long as I could, but you can only do that so long. Then I found that I was even initiating at times. Like in the morning or early afternoon—which for me made those first nondrinking sexual moments much easier and more enjoyable. They didn't trigger me to drink. And I am happy to report that it gets so much better. You start feeling so much more."

—MEG

"Wow! I'm smiling and thinking about how I will feel when I have sober sex. I really won't know till it happens. And I swear I'll be true to myself and not fake anything. That may end up being a good OR bad thing with my husband. I don't know."

—JK

"Better sex? How awesome! I have been fortunate to have an amazing love/sex partner for 43 years! The sex was always good. How much better might it have been without the anesthesia of alcohol? WOW! That's a sexy thought in itself, no regret involved."

—CAZZ

"Biggest milestone yet! Spent a week at my mountain house and went to the 'Saloon' Friday night. I'm known as a big wine-drinking party girl there among my friends. Didn't catch too much flack. My husband always complained that when I drank, he couldn't get me to go home. Well . . . stone-cold sober for the first time with my old buds and he still couldn't get me to leave! I had more fun than ever! And surprisingly the sex *was* amazing! Thank you, thank you, thank you, Annie!"

—ERIN

❚ DAY 14 ❚

Staying Mindful in the Midst of Chaos

In the midst of movement and chaos, keep stillness inside of you.
—DEEPAK CHOPRA

You've probably figured it out by now. This whole experiment is about mindfulness and becoming aware of ideas, thoughts, and actions that used to happen without your conscious knowledge or approval. It's easy to feel weak or hopeless when we keep having urges and desires to drink, especially if we give in to them. At this point in the experiment, awareness is the actual goal, not total abstinence.

Want to hear some good news? Becoming aware of your urges, even if you give in to them, can have a positive effect on how you respond to those urges days or weeks from now. When you stay present and mindful during a craving, you might be able to resist it in the moment. But even if you don't, you are still helping yourself in the long run.

Numerous studies show that when you try to repress or ignore an urge, you're actually making it worse. You're making it stronger. So, instead of running from it, turn around and face it head-on. Dive in and roll around in it. Become aware of all the feelings and emotions and physical sensations you're having during the craving. What is happening in your mind and in your body? I like to use a technique called Surfing the Urge. This technique was developed by Sarah Bowen, PhD, and Gordon Alan Marlatt, PhD, research scientists at the Addictive Behaviors Research Center at the University of Washington. Originally designed for studying smoking addiction, it works well for any cravings or urges.

Bowen and Marlatt gave a group of smokers a new package of their favorite cigarettes. Then they asked the smokers not to smoke for 12 hours before the study. By the time the group came in for the study, they were desperate for those cigarettes. Instead of giving in to the cravings right away, the researchers asked them to sit and do some very specific things. Look at the package of unopened cigarettes. Then wait a few minutes, being mindful of how they felt. Open the cellophane. Wait a few minutes and notice how they felt. Smell the cigarettes. Wait. Take one cigarette out and hold it. Wait. Take out a lighter. Wait. Light the lighter but not the cigarette. Wait. You get the point. The participants were present and mindful of their thoughts and feelings during each step of a process they would normally perform unconsciously.

▌ DISRUPT THE CYCLE

Neurologically, you're physically disrupting the craving cycle in your brain. It is possible to separate yourself from your addiction. And the more often you do it, the easier it becomes and the less tightly the addiction will grip you. And it works even if you give in! Those smokers all had that cigarette at the end of the study. They satisfied their cravings, which might look like a failure. In the following 24 hours, there was no real difference in their smoking behavior. But by 48 hours later, those smokers had cut back their cigarette consumption by 37 percent. It happened naturally and without struggle. They no longer lit up the second they felt the urge. And over time, it had a positive effect on how well they were able to resist those cravings.

TODAY, think of your craving as a wave. It builds and builds, applying more and more pressure, until it peaks. Then it gradually subsides until it disappears for a while. Similar to how the size and severity of an ocean wave depend on the weather and other environmental circumstances, your cravings will depend on the stress levels and other factors in your life. Sometimes your "crave wave" will be small and manageable. Other times it will seem like it's crashing down on you, and you're powerless to resist the undertow. No matter how powerful the urge, mindfulness is the key.

At whatever point you notice a craving, ask yourself these questions:

What was I thinking right before the craving started? What was I feeling? What was my emotional state?

What am I thinking and feeling right now? How does my body feel physically? Am I nervous, sweaty, or anxious?

Are these thoughts and feelings true?

Would I feel better not thinking these thoughts?

Don't try to stop thinking them; just ask the question. You're tickling your subconscious, that's all.

As a detached observer, you might find the next craving is a little less intense. Or you might find you can resist it for an hour, long enough to distract yourself with something fun. I'm not suggesting you should give in to the cravings, especially during the experiment. I am suggesting that even if you do have a drink, this technique is worthwhile, because the positive effects on your brain and behavior build up over time.

Day 14 Reflections from alcoholexperiment.com

"I used to drink because I was stressed. Since I've stopped drinking and already learned other coping tools like meditation, I hardly feel stressed anymore. Drinking causes the stress, but I just couldn't see it until I removed it from my life."

—AARON

"One of the reasons I'm doing this is because when my daughter asked me not to get a beer at a soccer game, I did anyway. I chose a drink over her earnest request. I even brought her up to the bar with me. I justified it to her as something I needed to relax. Immediately after getting the beer, the game started again and I took the beer to my seat. I realized I didn't even want it. I just wanted to drink with my friends at halftime. I bought it to fit in, to get that feeling of being the fun drinker. It was eye-opening. Now I tell her all the time that I'm not drinking anymore because she suggested it, and what a great idea that was. She's so proud, but more than that she's seeing that she matters more to me than a drink."

—MELISSA

"I am discovering that my use of alcohol is directly related to my uncomfortable feelings. I am essentially trying to escape myself and quiet down the chatter in my head. Somewhere along the line I learned that emotions shouldn't be tolerated, which is a lie. I am working on identifying my thoughts and emotions and then questioning their validity. I am trying to uncover what the real issue is behind my emotions. More often than not, it is a feeling of low self-worth and not being/doing enough, not being deserving of love unless I perform. I am getting so tired of this story. I have dragged this story around most of my life and I am ready to put it back on the shelf."

—EMILY

||| ACT #7 |||

Alcohol and Parenting
(a.k.a. Mommy Juice)

| AWARENESS

I remember so many times when I told my kids, "No, you can't have a sip. That is 'mommy juice.'" In fact, it's become such a well-used term that wine marketers have actually branded a line of wines "Mommy Juice." Both my husband and I were absolutely convinced that alcohol was a vital and necessary part of parenting. I remember getting him a Father's Day card one year that said "It's not drinking alone if the kids are home."

Let's name this belief:

"I need a drink to handle my kids."

But whether you're a parent or not, this section is incredibly powerful because what we're actually talking about is stress. Drinking to relieve intense stress. Parenting happens to be one form of stress that millions of people share, and the alcohol industry has latched on to that and targets parents, especially moms, as a market segment. So, if you're not a parent, read this through anyway and substitute your stressors. Maybe you're a college student trying to get through a rigorous semester. Maybe you have a high-pressure career. Whatever that stress is for you, the same addictive processes are happening in your brain.

Before we dive into deconstructing this belief, I want to tell you a story I learned from Allen Carr. He's an addiction expert who specializes in helping people quit smoking. He talks about a deadly meat-eating plant from the islands of the South Pacific called a pitcher plant. If you're an insect flying through the jungle and you catch a whiff of its amazing-smelling nectar, you are instantly attracted. You fly in closer, perch inside the rim, and start to drink. It's so tasty, and you're so focused on drinking, that you don't notice the gradual slope under your feet. And you begin to slide down toward the center of the plant. But you've got wings. You can fly out anytime. Just a couple more sips and you'll be off. The nectar is intoxicating—why not enjoy it? You deserve it, after all. Like all drinkers, you think you're totally in control and can leave at any time. But the slope gets steeper and steeper, and the darkness closes in around you. You try to stop drinking and fly away, but it's too late. The pitcher plant has you completely in its grasp. Eventually you stop drinking long enough to look down and make out a pool of dead bodies floating in the liquid. You're not drinking nectar—you're drinking the juice of other dead creatures. You are the drink.

As disgusting as that story is, it illustrates a point that we don't talk about enough. Alcohol is addictive, not only to some people—to *all* people. And we need to understand that something as innocent as having a glass of wine to get through making dinner for the kids can end up becoming a huge problem. The only way to get out of the trap is to avoid it altogether. And the only way to do that is to understand that alcohol is, indeed, a trap. Oftentimes addiction takes hold when we use a substance to relieve stress. And in our society today, there aren't many things more stressful than parenting, especially when the kids are young.

| CLARITY

Do you believe you need to drink to handle being a parent? I totally did. I thought I was relaxed and more present with kids. I thought if I had a glass of wine, I could play their games longer. Where did this come from? If you start paying attention, you'll see the messages all around you. The alcohol industry has targeted parents in a major way—everything from TV commercials to movies to social media memes. You can't scroll through Facebook for 15 seconds without seeing a post about alcohol and drinking to get through the day. We are telling ourselves this lie that we need to drink to deal with the kids. Here are some of the placards I've seen recently:

This margarita tastes like I don't even have kids.

The most expensive part of having kids is all the wine you have to drink.

Motherhood: Powered by love. Fueled by coffee. Sustained by wine.

Wine: The Duct Tape of Parenting.

Mom's happy meal: a Xanax and bottle of wine.

Dear children, You whine. I wine.

Homework: Turning parents into day-drinkers.

Alcohol branding has gotten out of control, with wines like Mad Housewife, Mommy's Time Out, and Mommy Juice. Marketers are actually targeting stressed-out moms with a substance that's only going to make things worse. Humorous Facebook pages and websites, such as Mommy Needs Vodka and Hurrah for Gin, are growing in popularity. This segment of the industry has seen a 25 percent surge in sales, which is huge growth. Parents are getting the message loud and clear—it's socially acceptable to drink away your stress.

The message is always presented as funny. But it's not. More than 40 percent of mothers say they drink to deal with parenting stress, and 30 percent say they've witnessed another mother drinking excessively on a playdate. As I write this, my heart breaks thinking about two women who emailed me in desperation because if they don't stop drinking, the court system is going to take away their children. These are smart, successful women. They volunteer, they have powerful careers, they help out with the PTA—and they are in big trouble. One of them received a DUI with her kids in the car. I know one mom who woke up from a blackout, and the last thing she could remember was being on a playdate with her toddler. She had *no idea* how she got home or how she had gotten her child into his crib for nap time. Talk about scary!

Parents are becoming so addicted to alcohol that they risk losing their kids. And we're making jokes about it.

As heartbreaking as that is for the parents, it's even worse for the children who have to witness their parents' embarrassing and dangerous behavior. It's worse for those little boys and girls who have to leave their parents and navigate a strange new world on their own, all because their mom or dad couldn't get it together.

This is harsh, I know. And I want you to understand that it's NOT FUNNY.

I also want you to know that it's not your fault. If you're a parent and you drink, you are in the pitcher plant. You probably feel like you can fly out, and it's not a big deal. But make no mistake: You are sliding down into the pool of decay. But once you understand what's happening in your brain when you drink to relieve stress, it's easier to resolve the cognitive dissonance around drinking and kids. And once you do that, you'll be able to push off and fly away from the temptation.

So let's look at the internal evidence first. Are you okay with how much you're drinking as a parent? I know I wasn't. I justified it. I made jokes about it, like the memes we see on social media. But I knew deep down it wasn't right. I can remember thinking, *How would we drive the kids to the hospital if we had to? We're both drunk.* I've heard countless stories of people who grew up with parents who drink. They were all so embarrassed by their loved ones' behavior that they swore they'd never be like that. Yet they come to me truly not knowing how they've become their parents. They're repeating the exact same behavior they witnessed as kids, and they feel powerless to stop it.

The statistics on alcohol and child abuse are tragic. But maybe you're not that bad. Maybe you only have a drink or two every now and then when the kids are particularly challenging. Children are incredibly perceptive. When you say, "Hang on, honey—I'll play with you as soon as I get a beer," they pick up on the subtle message that the drink is more important than they are. What words are you using with your kids, and what messages are you sending them? I can remember my own son telling me he didn't like it when my lips turned purple. That was a sign to him that I was changing into someone he didn't like, someone who was only half there. Children report that when their parents are drinking, it's like they aren't really there. They're distracted and only half paying attention.

We tell our kids that this is "Mommy's juice" and to do as we say, not as we do. But it's human nature to want what we can't have. So by withholding this magical liquid from our kids, they are being trained to want it more. Studies show that children who grow up seeing their parents drunk are three times more likely to have problems with alcohol and drugs. They have more eating disorders. And they're four times more likely to suffer from depression. Some parents offer sips of alcohol to their kids to prevent the "forbidden allure" of something for grown-ups. But research is showing that these same kids are actually *more* likely to drink as adults. We're subconsciously conditioning our own children to believe that they cannot handle life without alcohol. Is that true? Is that what you want for them?

How will our children believe us when we tell them about the dangers of alcohol if we're drinking ourselves? When they're eventually told that it's addictive and can rob you of your memories and health, they're going to worry about us. Or they won't believe the facts because Mom and Dad wouldn't drink if it was really dangerous. I remember learning about how cigarettes cause cancer and being terrified for my parents and the people I cared about who smoked.

Each of these ACT Technique chapters are trying to undo some subconscious belief you adopted growing up. Are you unknowingly setting your own kids up to have the same misguided beliefs about alcohol?

Okay, let's talk about the external evidence and what's actually happening in your body. When I first started drinking, it was a fun social experience. But over time, it turned into something I felt I desperately needed, especially after my second son was born. It was a stressful time in my life when I was traveling for work every other week. I felt guilty because I wasn't home. And when I was home, my husband worked long into the night after the kids were in bed. Wine was more than just a fun way to relax; it became my friend and ally. It wasn't something I wanted. It was something I thought I *needed*.

Here's the thing—it wasn't my fault. And if you're in the same boat, it's not your fault, either. Your body is trying to help you survive. Dr. Kevin McCauley has spent his career studying the brain science behind addiction, and he talks about something called the hedonic system. It's the part of our brain that pursues pleasure as a means of survival. Remember that your brain is *always* seeking survival above everything else, right? And interestingly, intense stress can be seen by your brain as a serious threat.

Here's how it works: Your hedonic system runs off a baseline reading. In times of severe stress, that baseline goes up and things that used to be pleasurable, like taking a walk or reading a book, don't cut it anymore and you need something more to lower your stress levels. And that means you're more likely to reach for alcohol or another addictive substance to relieve the stress. By drinking to relieve stress, from parenting or anything else, you've literally rewired your brain to believe that's the only way you can survive it. You're stuck in the pitcher plant. People will say, "Just stop drinking, for heaven's sake. You're about to lose your kids!" But it's not that simple. Your evolutionary mind now overrides your common sense. Survival trumps all, and your brain equates alcohol with survival. You literally cannot resist when it gets to this point. Your brain tells you that you actually *need it to survive.*

Throughout history and in all parts of the world, people handle parenting just fine without alcohol. So, we're not born with this need to drink to handle stress. We're *conditioned over time* to believe it. All the jokes and social media memes we read and share are sending the message loud and clear. Our own parents might have perpetuated the message. We're telling ourselves we can't handle it. We're not resilient enough. We're weak. When we do that, we're giving away our power to alcohol.

But before you come down on yourself (like I know I did), please remember we are all doing the best we can, and making the best decisions we know how to make with the information we have. Until you read this chapter, maybe the only information you had was a funny joke you heard or your own experience that dealing with the kids is easier when you drink. But now you know the truth. You've been fed false information. You've been tricked into thinking that alcohol makes life simpler, when in fact it's the opposite.

You now have new information.

You understand what's happening with your hedonic system.

You are aware of what your drinking is doing to your kids.

And you are making a great new choice. As you take this 30-day break from alcohol, you have the opportunity to become more mindful and to decide whether you want to go in a different direction. So do the best you can with this new information.

▌TURNAROUND

The opposite of "*I need a drink to handle my kids*" or "*I am a better parent when I drink*" is "*I don't need a drink to handle my kids*" or "*I am a worse parent when I drink*." Come up with as many ways as you can that the opposite is as true as or truer in your life than the original belief.

❙ DAY 15 ❙

Social Life and Dating

Be bold, be brave enough to be your true self.
—QUEEN LATIFAH

❙ SOCIAL SKILLS

Look, social skills are exactly that—skills. You need to learn and practice them to get good at them. So many of us start drinking at a young age, and we never develop the skills to feel confident talking in social settings with new people or going on a date without alcohol. We don't crack bad jokes and learn how to recover. We don't get shot down and move on. We don't experience heartbreak without the numbing effects of a drink to make us feel better. It takes practice. If we were all perfect at everything from the moment we're born, what would be the point? Life is all about experimentation and growth.

The good news is that it's never too late to learn how to interact socially with confidence, even if you'd prefer to be home alone with a book. But don't put pressure on yourself. Don't expect that you'll find your soul mate right out of the gate. Give yourself the gift of making mistakes without judgment. It's okay to dance crazy and be expressive while you're sober. People like it. They admire it, and they wish they could do it. The best part is you'll remember it later. If it was a good experience, you'll cherish the memory. If it was a bad experience, you can learn from it and grow your social skill set.

Small talk can be stressful. And no matter how extroverted you are, walking into a room full of strangers is often nerve racking. It's a common human experience, and very natural, to feel uncomfortable meeting and socializing with new people. It is believed that this mechanism of initial discomfort around strangers helped protect us when we lived in a more tribal society. It ensured we were cautious as we got to know others and would not say or do anything that would lead to discord among tribes. Alcohol seems to provide the perfect solution, but with all sorts of icky consequences. So instead of alcohol, here's an easy way to engage people in conversation without feeling awkward—ask questions! Seriously, the question mark is the introvert's best friend. Get the other person talking and you won't have to do all the work. How was their day? What did they do for lunch? What job would they have if they didn't have to make money? What hobbies do they enjoy? Where did they grow up? How many siblings do they have? Where did their grandparents grow up? It goes on and on. You could spend an entire evening without having to talk about yourself at all. Of course, whoever you are talking to is probably going to ask you questions, too. But it's so much more comfortable to answer a direct question than it is to come up with awkward small talk. And the truth is that being genuinely curious about others is both fun and rewarding.

DATING WITHOUT DRINKING

If you're single, you might be thinking there's no way you'll be able to meet people or go out on dates during this experiment. Maybe you rely on alcohol to make you funnier or feel more attractive. Maybe drinking is the only way you have enough courage to go out and talk to strangers in social situations. Or maybe you feel like no one could ever be attracted to you without the wit and charm you think comes from a bottle.

So maybe during this experiment you practice caring for yourself a bit more. Look in the mirror. What qualities do you like the most? Do you have a killer set of biceps? Are your ankles shapely? Or do you have an amazing smile that can light up a room? Focus on what you love about yourself, and others will be drawn to you. We think loving ourselves means thinking our bodies are sexy or thinking we are smart enough, good enough, etc., when really we should be learning to love ourselves as we love our children. Because they exist. Love your body because it keeps you alive. Take care of it because it is what takes care of you. Treat it tenderly because you care for it like you would a child. You don't love your kids because they are attractive enough. You love them because they are your kids. Again, we didn't create ourselves, so what right do we have to treat ourselves so badly.

Make Your Own Dating Rules

Next, let's examine this assumption: *Drinking is the only way I have enough courage to go out and talk to strangers.* Okay, the first thing to know about yourself is whether you are an introvert or an extrovert. Some people just aren't wired to hit the party circuit and hook up with people they don't know. Our culture idolizes the extroverts, the people who crave social interaction. But a full 50 percent of people are actually introverts. They would much prefer to interact with one or two friends in a low-key setting. If that's you, great! Don't force yourself to be something you're not. I'm not suggesting you can't ever meet new people or go out on first dates. I'm saying you can do it in a way that feels more comfortable. If you have to have alcohol to meet people, maybe you need a different approach. Instead of going to big, boozy parties with loud music, try taking up a hobby and joining a club full of people interested in the same things. Maybe you join a rock-climbing gym or a country club where you can sign up to meet people on the golf course. Who made the rule that a first date is always "meeting for a drink"? You can make up your own rules. A date could be taking a class together, or volunteering together, or having coffee on a Sunday morning. Be unconventional. It's cool!

Alcohol and Attraction

I feel more attractive once I am buzzed. I can let loose and stop fo-cusing on my flaws. Guess what? Even though you might feel more attractive, the opposite is happening. It's easy to believe alcohol is helping because your inhibitions are lowered and other drunk people around you have dulled their senses with alcohol, too. But if 100 peo-ple are drinking heavily, 80 of them wish they could enjoy themselves with less booze. This might surprise you, but when people are looking for a partner, they find minimal alcohol consumption much more at-tractive. Even when I was drinking I tended to respect nondrinkers and felt they would make better partners and parents. I secretly thought it was so badass when someone said, "I don't drink." A pretty girl or a hot guy who has self-confidence without drinking? Super-attractive.

TODAY, think about an alternative way to meet new people. One that's comfortable and easy. Or if you're already in a committed rela-tionship, think about how you can take your partner out on a date where alcohol doesn't enter into the equation. Could you go on a midday bike ride and picnic? Could you find a lake and go swimming at midnight? Get yourself outside the usual "dinner, drinks, and a movie" date mode and surprise yourself! If you're in different sur-roundings, engaging in different activities, there's a chance you won't even think about adding alcohol to the mix. And anytime you catch yourself feeling awkward, ask a question. That's sure to take the pres-sure off and get the conversation flowing again.

Day 15 Reflections from alcoholexperiment.com

"Day 15 and going strong. I have been lucky so far in that I have not been in a social situation where I have to make small talk with strangers. That will change soon, and it will be very interesting to see how I respond, because in the past I have always used alcohol to feel comfortable."   —JOYCE

"Day 15 AF. Feeling good and I'm finally sleeping through the night now. I'm no longer having physical cravings for alcohol, but sometimes still have what I call 'routine cravings,' which is when I perform a task that I used to associate with alcohol (such as watching TV or movies or just relaxing on the patio in the evenings). During these moments it just feels like something is missing, but I'm not missing alcohol at all, or its negative effects, and look forward to creating a new routine for myself AF."   —RUSSELL

"I can recall wanting to get my drink on before meeting a new person so that talkative, personable me could feel comfortable to come out and play. Sober me, overthinking me, quiet me didn't seem like someone a new person would like. Drinking did feel like a way to get out of my head and be able to talk and to meet and to drop all the judgmental stuff that goes on in my head sober. What happened, though, I can see now, is there was a loss of connection to the other person. The connection I felt was more illusion than reality. I was so concerned with being personable, I forgot to be real. Drinking allowed me to chat up my first husband at a bar. If I was sober, I would have never even wanted to get to know him. He would have bored me to tears. I divorced him after five years. But can I really say not marrying him would have made my life better? We have a great daughter. I learned about myself. Maybe I can say this: Had I not been drinking, not chatting up a boy I would have never otherwise chatted up or been attracted to, I may have saved myself years of grief. I can now appreciate raw, uncomfortable, sober weird-feeling moments that have not been smoothed over by the easy-breezy flow of alcohol. Is the awkward moment something to embrace instead of fear? Yes, I think it is."

—ALEXIS

❚ DAY 16 ❚

The Power of Belief

Beliefs have the power to create and the power to destroy.
Human beings have the awesome ability to take any experience
of their lives and create a meaning that disempowers them
or one that can literally save their lives.
—TONY ROBBINS

You've heard this before, and you'll hear it again: Your mind is incredibly powerful. It can be a staunch ally or your worst enemy, depending on how you use it. The good news is that once you learn how the mind works, you can take control and use its power to change anything in your life. If you believe that you're going to be miserable without a drink in your hand at a social occasion, sporting event, concert, or even home alone, you will be. If you believe you're going to be lonely, you will be. If you believe you're going to be bored, you will be. If you believe this experiment is miserable, it will be.

I'm not asking you to counter these beliefs. Simply thinking, *I believe I will be happy without alcohol*, isn't enough. That's using willpower, and we all know that willpower doesn't last in the long term. Worse, your brain knows you're lying to it. You have to actually *believe* what you're telling yourself. So, how do you make that happen? Can you actually install new beliefs like you're installing software on your computer? Absolutely! When you start to question your beliefs, you create space in your mind for new beliefs to be installed.

| CONDITIONING

Let's talk about conditioning for a moment. Neuropsychologists agree that we spend our lifetimes being conditioned. We're teaching our brains what to expect in any circumstance. Whether what we expect actually happens doesn't matter, because we will manufacture circumstances that deliver exactly what we expect. This phenomenon has been studied over and over again. As we just learned, if you expect to be miserable, you will be. If you expect that going alcohol free for 30 days won't be that big of a deal, it won't be. The ACT Technique is designed to help decondition you—to change your beliefs and what you expect. Once you shake the foundations of those conditioned beliefs, you can start to move forward without being hindered by unhelpful and unhealthy beliefs.

A major fear for people before they start the Alcohol Experiment is that they won't be able to do it. They don't believe it will be possible to stop drinking, even for a short time, because of whatever their circumstance is. They don't believe it will be possible to be alcohol free and happy at the same time. Or alcohol free and relaxed at the same time. That's a completely understandable fear, but it's based on a false belief. Once you start to see other people being successful, you start to believe you can be successful, too. This is what's so great about the Alcohol Experiment community. You get to see other people who are alcohol-free and happy. They're making it. And you can, too.

Confirmation Bias

So you know you're being conditioned to believe certain things and expect certain things in life. But you also help cement those beliefs into your mind with something called confirmation bias. Have you ever tried to look something up online and stopped looking once you found an article or a website that confirmed what you thought? Take dietary fat, for instance. There are plenty of studies and articles and forums out there that claim fat is bad for you. There are just as many that claim the exact opposite. So which do you believe? You believe what you've been conditioned to believe, unless you're consciously trying to change that conditioning.

Confirmation bias doesn't only happen when we're surfing the net or browsing social media. When drinking becomes uncomfortable for us, we develop cognitive dissonance. The mind is uncomfortable because we're wrestling with two conflicting ideas—alcohol relaxes us versus alcohol is making us miserable. That dissonance is incredibly painful, so the brain looks for ways to ease the pain. How? By looking for confirmation one way or the other. Maybe we share social media posts about the benefits of red wine. That confirms wine is good for us, and so the dissonance is eased. Maybe we put funny plaques on the wall, like "Gone drinking. Will return when I can't remember why I started." What that does is make us feel better because it's funny, but subconsciously it also makes us feel weak because it's confirming our belief that we need alcohol to deal with our lives.

Recently, I've noticed more and more slogans that are supposed to be funny but really aren't. "I'm not addicted to wine. We're just in a very committed relationship." And "A day without wine is like . . . just kidding, I have no idea." These plaques are for sale for women to put up in their kitchens. The truth is that we're justifying an addiction. We're using confirmation bias to justify heavier and heavier amounts of drinking.

Visualization

Now you know the ways you reinforce your beliefs. What are some ways you can go about breaking and reconstructing them? One of my favorite ways is to use visualization. I know that might sound a little woo-woo, but stick with me here. Numerous studies show that the mind can't tell the difference between a real memory and a powerfully visualized memory. One strong visualization to try is to picture yourself going out and having a great time without alcohol.

When I first gave up drinking I would visualize the entire evening. I'd imagine myself going out for the evening with some friends. I would imagine the restaurant we were going to. I'd imagine ordering a big steak dinner and, instead of the usual bottle of wine, visualize ordering a tonic and lime. And then I'd visualize myself laughing and laughing and having a great time. It worked! The brain can't tell the difference, because when it has colorful, vivid, convincing pictures, it essentially tries to make those pictures a reality. So those visualizations are actually affecting your future reality. How cool is that?

One mistake people make is to think about and visualize what we *don't want*. But the mind doesn't necessarily understand the word *don't*—you get whatever you think about. Which, in this case, is the opposite of what you do want. So if you imagine, *I don't want to just sit there being miserable*, but you're thinking of yourself sitting there miserable, that's what your brain works from. It tries to make that scenario a reality. But if you think of yourself going out and having a great time, your brain tries to make *that* scenario a reality.

Just saying it out loud doesn't work. You have to visualize all the nuances—the entire scene. And be as specific as you possibly can when you visualize. Mentally rehearse what you're wearing, what you're thinking, and what you're saying. Take the time to sit for five or six minutes, set a timer, close your eyes, and go through the visualization. And don't worry and think, *What if this doesn't work?* Try it. Be as specific as possible.

If you want to boost the effects even further, add emotions to your visualization. How will you *feel* going out to dinner and ordering an iced tea? *I'm going to feel amazing. I'll feel so in control of myself and so proud that I'm having so much fun without alcohol.* Then try to feel the feelings in the moment while you're visualizing. Get that excited feeling in your chest. Feel the tingling in your hands. Put that big smile on your face. The more emotions you visualize, the more powerful your visualizations will be.

TODAY, think of the next stressful thing you're going to go through when you might be tempted to give in and have a drink.

Maybe it's going out with your friends. Maybe it's just surviving another stressful day at work. Then go through the visualization exercise above and visualize the experience exactly how *you want it to go*. Make some notes about the visualization in your journal. Then after the event, come back and write down what actually happened. Did you get what you expected? Did your visualization come true?

Day 16 Reflections from alcoholexperiment.com

"Wow, I'm so stoked! This is the longest I've been alcohol-free in probably a year and a half. I'm thrilled to have broken the cycle and to be creating new healthy habits and altering my neural pathways. My husband discreetly had a few drinks last night. I could smell it on him. He was respectful and was not obvious or drunk. The best thing is, I didn't desire to join him. I didn't even ask or bring it up. I'm too content with the changes I've made for myself and the future to fall back into the bottle."   —CAMI

"Day 16 and I'm so proud of myself. I feel alive and present in this wonderful life! Keep going—it gets better!"   —REGINA

"I used visualization and made it through my first event AF. Turning down wine/beer was easier than I thought. At the same time, I do struggle thinking about how I'll get through this summer. I waffle between thinking my problem is 'not that bad' and yet I have tried to stop drinking four times in the past five years. It may not be 'that bad,' but I'm uncomfortable with it and I want more out of life. I know that overall, it's not going to enhance my health in the long run. I definitely have my good and bad days, only about 16 AF now. I really would love for this to be my last attempt. I cannot wait until being AF is automatic and as easy as being a nonsmoker. I keep reminding myself I kicked the cigs. Here's to the day when to drink/not drink isn't even an issue because I just don't care that I don't drink!"   —BAILEY

||| ACT #8 |||

Alcohol Is My Friend

| AWARENESS

"Alcohol helps when I am feeling lonely."

Many people feel like they're less lonely when they drink. It's like even if their friends don't understand them, "Uncle Jack" (Jack Daniel's whiskey) and "Old Grand-Dad" (bourbon whiskey) totally get them. It seems to keep loneliness away. I know this was true for me.

| CLARITY

You probably do feel less alone when you drink. And at some point, you might have had a bad day and decided to try drinking alone. There's no one watching you when you drink by yourself, so you can drink a lot quickly. You don't have a social situation to slow you down. So your blood alcohol content rises fast and you feel that quick hit of happiness right away. It feels euphoric for that first 30 minutes or so.

Naturally, when you've experienced this firsthand, the belief that alcohol fights off loneliness settles into your subconscious and makes itself at home. And when you drink to overcome pain, the alcohol actually has a more pronounced effect, because it is a numbing agent, than when you drink for pleasure. So what's actually going on?

That first feeling of euphoria takes away any discomfort you were feeling earlier—the very discomfort that made you decide to have that drink. And you probably feel pretty good being alone, maybe for the first time in a long time. For most people, being alone isn't fun. It's awkward and uncomfortable. But when you add alcohol, suddenly it's great. So of course you feel like it's the booze that's fighting off the loneliness. It's nothing more than a chemical concoction, yet you can even start to develop a friendlike relationship with it. It's not that alcohol is your friend, it's that you feel the pain of loneliness less when you're drinking.

Let me ask you some questions, though. Since you started drinking alone, has your life become more or less solitary? In my experience, I looked forward to drinking, and when I was drinking alone, I could do it pretty much whenever I wanted. One woman told me she knew something needed to change when she started looking forward to her evening glass of wine even more than her kids coming home from school.

Has your life become more social or less social since you started drinking alone? It's normal for people to start avoiding social situations, even ones where they used to drink with their friends, because they figure out they can drink as much as they want at home with no one judging them. And they don't even have to deal with people— bonus! Soon you might find reasons to excuse yourself from any social situation so you can drink alone.

Are you closer to or further away from the people you love? Your children. Your partner. I thought my drinking brought me closer to my partner because I could unwind around him. But over the years, as I increased my drinking, I often found myself in bed with a glass of wine when he was downstairs watching TV. The alcohol actually drove us apart.

Is drinking the only social activity your friends seem to do these days? You might be feeling lonely because alcohol is the only shared experience you have anymore. I remember when I stopped drinking, a dear lifelong friend I'd known since kindergarten stopped coming over to hang out. It was a long time before I finally found out that she didn't think we'd have anything to talk about or do if we weren't drinking margaritas together. This took me by surprise. I had no idea she felt like that. I'd known her for over 30 years, and we'd only been drinking together for the past 10. Even though we had a huge shared history, she had this overwhelming fear because recently we had only alcohol in common. She was worried that it would be awkward. I told her that every new experience without alcohol took a little while to get used to and asked her to come over. If it was awkward or uncomfortable, well, at least we'd get a good laugh out of it.

She came over for the first time in two years. And we had the best time together! We talked about our families and politics and religion. We laughed until our stomachs hurt. We had so much fun connecting with each other that we completely forgot about the movie and hike we had planned. And now we're closer than we've ever been. All because we showed up and connected to each other. That was something that alcohol had been stealing from us all along, and we didn't even know it.

Let's look at the external evidence for a minute. There are actual physiological reasons that alcohol robs us of our ability to connect with other people. Alcohol slows down the speed your neurons fire in your brain. This means you think more slowly. You take longer to respond. And the longer the alcohol is in your system, the harder you have to concentrate just to speak at all. You don't retain much of what's happening around you. So you retreat further and further into yourself. Alcohol blurs the edges around what's actually going on. You also become emotionally withdrawn.

Here's something to try during this experiment. Go out with a bunch of your friends while they're drinking (and you're not). Then try to have a real heart-to-heart conversation with them. You'll find it's nearly impossible to get them to take you seriously. You can see it in their eyes that they're not entirely present. They're distracted. Maybe they're too quick to laugh or respond, like they're trying too hard. If this behavior surprises you, realize you never noticed it before because you were drinking, too. You were also withdrawn into your own little world. I didn't notice any of this until I stopped drinking. How can two people form a true and lasting connection when they're both worried about falling off their chairs? You have to have other times when you're not drinking with your friends if you want to experience a true connection and dispel any feelings of loneliness.

Real human connection comes from being vulnerable. Researcher Brené Brown has centered her life's work on this idea. Think about it. When people seem completely put together and perfect, do you want to connect with them? Probably not. You might want to be like them, but you don't want to reach out and talk to them. That comes only when a person is vulnerable and shows their flaws as well as their strengths. Yet we try to pretend we're perfect all the time. We think if we pretend we're GREAT, then people will want to be friends with us. But it's only when we admit when we are hurt or disappointed—when we're NOT perfect—that people connect and our loneliness subsides. Even if you and your best friend experience a drunken moment of weeping—and a confessional "I love you, man!"—chances are pretty good that neither of you will remember it in the morning. Alcohol makes you think you're connecting, when you're really withdrawn.

If we truly want to combat loneliness, we need to be courageous enough to be raw and real. We need to talk about our struggles. The more I show up with my real stories, the more people come back with their own real stories. We're all struggling together. The more we pretend we have it all together, the more we push other people away. Drinking Annie was pretty good at small talk and making the jokes, but she wasn't great at making lasting connections. In fact, despite the perceived closeness and the fact that we poured out all our drunken secrets to one another, the people I drank with most were not people

I felt I could call on if I was having a hard time. As alcohol steals our ability to connect, the more alone we become. It masquerades as our best friend, and all our relationships become superficial. No one is truly themselves after even a few drinks, and we lose the ability to be truly vulnerable. We lose our chance for real, true relationships.

As my drinking progressed, I found that it isolated me more and more. The more embarrassed I became about my struggle, the more worried I was about people judging me, and the more I wanted to be alone with the bottle. Drinking often starts out as a social activity, but then it becomes something that we do alone and sometimes even in secret, driving us further and further away from true human connection.

TURNAROUND

The opposite of *"alcohol is my friend"* is *"alcohol is not my friend"* or *"alcohol is my enemy."* Come up with as many ways as you can that the opposite is as true as or truer in your life than the original belief.

Relieving Boredom Without Drinking

Boredom leads to creativity.
Imagination is more important than knowledge.
—ALBERT EINSTEIN

If drinking used to be a major activity for you, this experiment might leave you with more time on your hands than you thought it would. That is a great thing! Yet you might feel a bit bored, so let's explore that emotion today. Interestingly, boredom is one of the top reasons that people go back to drinking. It's important to get a handle on this uncomfortable emotion so it can't undermine your experiment.

Boredom can be a loaded topic, especially when it involves other people. There's a lot of implied guilt and blame involved, as you'll soon discover. The common belief among regular drinkers is that alcohol relieves their boredom and makes boring people easier to tolerate. But when you get right down to it, what is boredom? We might define it as a disinterest in the world around us or even in our own thoughts. It's like saying our lives are not enough for us. That being alive is not enough; we need something else. The concept of boredom is nothing new. References to it appeared in ancient Pompeii as early as the first century AD. I imagine it's probably been around since humans first existed.

Boredom is an incredibly uncomfortable state for many people. Scientists studied this by putting people in a room for 15 minutes to be alone with their thoughts. The only other item in the room was a device they could push to give themselves an electric shock. Eighty percent of the people decided to shock themselves and cause pain rather than sit and be bored. One person actually shocked himself 180 times! We brush boredom off as this trivial thing that we should be able to simply snap out of, but researchers are finding that it's not trivial at all, and there are some fascinating connections between boredom and addiction to substances like alcohol.

When we're young, we're taught to feel guilty about being bored. I remember my dad telling me that boredom doesn't exist and it was all in my head. In school, children are often told to stop complaining or that they're weak-willed and unimaginative if they're bored. Some parents say, "Only boring people get bored," or "If you're bored, I'll give you something to do!" (Of course, that thing is always unpleasant, like cleaning your room or taking out the trash.) And over time, we learn to be ashamed of this state of boredom.

So we have this feeling that we don't know what to do about, and our parents, teachers, and other authority figures tell us we shouldn't be feeling it. That sets us up for classic cognitive dissonance. We feel bad or embarrassed that we're bored, so we seek out ways to change our state of mind. Some people eat. Some people mindlessly scan social media. And many of us reach for a drink. For a short time, alcohol numbs the boredom and the guilt we feel about being bored in the first place.

Back in 1986, psychologists at the University of Oregon developed a test to study boredom. It's called the Boredom Proneness Scale, and you can actually take it online. It's not surprising that people who are easily bored are more prone to addiction. Teenagers who report being easily bored are 50 percent more likely to try drinking, illegal drugs, or smoking. Think back for a moment. Have you always been prone to boredom? Or did you have creative activities to engage in? What were they? How did you handle boredom before you started drinking?

It's important to understand that boredom isn't always a bad thing. I read a study where doctors put participants inside an MRI machine.

When they reported feeling bored, there was a 5 percent drop in their overall brain activity. But there were huge increases in activity in certain areas, specifically the parts of the brain that recall autobiographical facts, the part that seeks self-knowledge, and the creative center where hypothetical situations are invented. All those creative parts of the brain were much more active, even though the overall activity was lower. Interesting, isn't it? Boredom may well be responsible for all the great works of art and literature, your favorite movies, and technological innovations. Albert Einstein was a notoriously bored person. Legend has it that his famous theory of relativity came about when he was particularly bored in an algebra class and was imagining that he could escape by being faster than a beam of light. What amazing things do you have inside you that are waiting to be shared with the world?

Some people believe that true bliss and contentment actually happen on the other side of boredom. They believe that boredom is a sublime emotion, something to be savored and appreciated. In fact, researchers are urging parents not to fill their kids' summer schedules with activity. They suggest setting kids up in situations where they will be bored in order to foster their ability to be still in their emotions. Children need to develop the ability to pay attention to the little things that bring lasting joy. It's a skill we're robbing our children of by providing constant on-demand entertainment.

Of course, beyond a certain point, boredom becomes unhealthy. Studies show that when people (and animals) are bored too long, they can actually go insane. When you're drunk, you aren't capable of feeling boredom because you've numbed your senses and emotions. Boredom is your brain telling you it needs to be stimulated. So think of some ways to do that.

My favorite ways to relieve boredom involve activities where I'm striving to reach a goal. Since my husband and I started tae kwon do, we're always working to improve our skills and move from white belt through the colored belts; eventually we hope to earn our black belts. Sustained growth and achievement is built right in. Happiness is often found in areas of growth. Maybe you want to write a novel and you can check off the chapters as they're completed. Even something as simple as walking can give you a sense of achievement. Try a GPS app to track your daily miles as you walk the distance it would take to make it to Rome. Celebrate with a big Italian dinner party when you reach virtual Rome.

When you're drunk, everything feels the same. Whether you're eating a nice dinner, you're at a concert, or you're home watching Netflix, it's all the same numb, fuzzy feeling. Every single experience you have feels exactly the same. After I gave up drinking, I saw that life has so much variety to offer, and we need all our senses intact in order to experience it. When we take the time to appreciate it, life without alcohol is the opposite of boring.

And what about the belief that drinking makes other people more interesting? My answer to that is to ask why you're with those people in the first place. I certainly understand needing to be at a business or networking function where you don't want to be. And I did my fair share of drinking to deal with people I had no interest in. But when I did that, I robbed myself of the ability to form true connections with people who might be worth getting to know if I gave them a chance. When you drink to make someone else more interesting, you're the one getting cheated. You're poisoning yourself just so you can be around someone you don't want to be around in the first place. I've found that if I pay attention, I can usually find something worth knowing about everyone. And if I really can't stand someone, I can politely excuse myself and go find someone else to talk to. I don't need a drink to do that.

So what do you think? While it's true that alcohol does temporarily relieve boredom by slowing down your brain, it also numbs your ability to experience and appreciate the things that bring you joy. Given what you now know about the creative centers in your brain lighting up during periods of boredom, are you more likely to put up with those uncomfortable emotions to see what's on the other side? Imagine what might emerge!

TODAY, remember that boredom has a purpose. Turning it off robs you and the world of something beautiful and important that only you can offer. Try, just for now, to sit with your boredom. Let it wash over you. Allow the discomfort. And see what happens.

Then make a list of all the activities you'd like to try someday. Don't hold yourself back or put anything off-limits. Want to go skydiving or drive race cars? Add them to the list. Want to quit your job and start your own business? Great! How about taking up ballroom dancing or shipwreck diving? Spend some creative energy making up a long, wild list. Then start thinking about which activity you want to do first and go do it! Even if all you do is research it a little on the internet, it's a start.

You have something amazing inside you that's just waiting to be created. Boredom is your brain crying out for stimulation. You simply need a healthy kind of stimulation.

Day 17 Reflections from alcoholexperiment.com

"I can relate to the boredom. Boredom has always been with me and I always answered with, 'Hey, a beer sounds good!' or 'Let's get a little wine,' or 'How about a cocktail?' I felt a lot of tension last night, I think due to my unanswered boredom. My wife was having her wine and I was drinking water, which was not a problem. The tension was coming from boredom. I didn't know it at the time, but it makes perfect sense now. . . . This is an excellent learning adventure! There is some discomfort, there is some pain, but seeing my old lifelong friend Al Cohol being exposed for the backstabbing, toxic, miserable substance that he really is, that is refreshing, exciting, hopeful, and motivating. I can't wait to keep living this life!"   —TIM

"I found that alcohol was keeping me unfocused and scattered and afraid to tackle the things I want to do. I am coming out of that fog. All I want now is to push myself in ways that I never have before. Alcohol for me was a lot about fear and lack of confidence, and this is starting to change. I feel great today."   —BRYCE

"Woke up this morning feeing euphoric. Couldn't wait to start the day. I can't remember the last time I felt this good for more than a day at a time. There have been so, so many years of wine-filled evenings leaving me exhausted and disappointed. I used to be a morning person, optimistic and energetic, but in the last few years I've become down and blue and lethargic—struggling to get through the dull day until 7:00 p.m. when I can have that first glass. I really think I lost myself in the blur. The last 17 days have been a revelation. I think the old me is on his way back."

—JULIAN

▌ DAY 18 ▌

Why Tolerance Is Literally a Buzzkill

Happiness is not a matter of intensity
but of balance and order and rhythm and harmony.
—THOMAS MERTON

▌ THE SCIENCE BEHIND TOLERANCE

Do you believe that a high alcohol tolerance is a good thing? I used to. People would make fun of me and say I was a "cheap date" because I got drunk so quickly. I didn't like that, so I consciously tried to increase my tolerance so I could keep up with my coworkers. Other people consider high tolerance a bad thing and consciously try to decrease their tolerance so they can get drunk faster and not have to spend so much money for the same buzz.

Alcohol tolerance is your body's way of trying to regulate itself in the midst of confusing signals and chaos. Let's look at the brain science, so you can see what's actually going on when you consume alcohol. Your brain has what's called a "pleasure circuit," and it's made up of the prefrontal cortex, the nucleus accumbens, and the ventral tegmental area (VTA). Alcohol affects your prefrontal cortex and makes you feel less inhibited. It gives you a temporary feeling of pleasure. Unfortunately, the more impaired your prefrontal cortex becomes, the less you're able to say no to that next drink. You're also less able to resist the dumb things you think about doing or saying. An impaired prefrontal cortex is why people drive when they shouldn't. You've damaged the part of your brain responsible for good judgment. After all, that's what your inhibitions are.

As the alcohol hits your system, the VTA stimulates dopamine release. Dopamine helps you feel pleasure. One of the main areas of your brain that actually registers enjoyment is the nucleus accumbens. It's not surprising that addictive substances stimulate these areas of the brain more effectively than everyday pleasures, such as taking a walk with your dog, watching a movie, or enjoying a good meal. In fact, addictive substances stimulate pleasure chemicals far beyond normal levels. That might sound great at first, but remember that your body is always trying to protect you by maintaining homeostasis. It wants to keep you in balance.

After drinking, your inhibitions are low and your pleasure chemicals are unnaturally high. A part of your brain realizes that no good can come of that, if left unchecked. So, as I explained earlier, it releases a counter-chemical called dynorphin. When you've got too many pleasurable endorphins racing through your system, your brain releases a sedative. Dynorphin counteracts the endorphins.

Now, if your brain had to do this only once, it might be okay. You feel high for a little while, cue the dynorphin, then you come back down and that's the end of it. Unfortunately, we all want to keep that happy-go-lucky feeling, and our inhibitions are lowered. So as soon as we feel ourselves coming back down, we order another drink. The alcohol brings you back up, but not as high as you were previously. Your brain says, "Uh-oh," and releases even more dynorphin to bring you back down. This time, you go even lower than earlier. You bring yourself back up with another drink, and your brain reacts with another hit of dynorphin. As you become more and more numb, the endorphins don't work as well, and you never rise to the same level you were at just one drink ago.

The cycle looks like this:

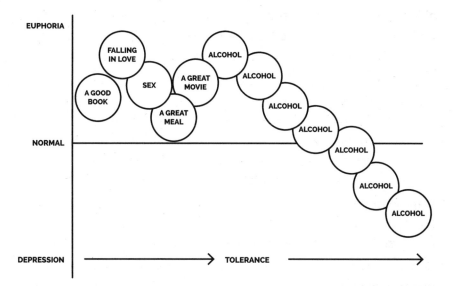

Each subsequent drink brings you lower and lower until you fall well below the baseline of happiness you started with. This is why happy drunks often wind up crying at the end of the night.

It's a neurological fact that the more alcohol you consume, the lower your pleasure dips until you are much worse off than you were when you started. Does that sound like fun to you?

Decreased Tolerance for Fun

There's even worse news, though, because your brain is smart. When drinking for fun becomes a habit, like hitting happy hour every day after work, it can predict exactly when and how much dynorphin it needs to release. So it prereleases the stuff! It takes proactive measures to protect your life. This is how tolerance builds up. You need more alcohol to even feel that first release of endorphins because your brain has already released the countermeasure. Bummer.

When your pleasure levels are artificially stimulated on a consistent basis, your brain gets used to it. And soon, you find you can no longer enjoy normal, everyday activities that used to make you happy. Spending time with your kids, walking your dog, painting, playing games—none of that offers enough pleasure anymore. Your fun becomes entirely dependent on a substance that your brain has to work hard to keep from killing you.

Dynorphin affects the pleasure you get from *everything*. That means when you build a tolerance for alcohol, you're also building a tolerance for sex, and laughter, and ice cream! Anything you used to find pleasing doesn't do it for you anymore. You have to return to using alcohol (or whatever your drug of choice is) in higher and higher quantities until you become more and more focused on your next drink. Eventually, everyday pleasures don't even register anymore. That IS a big deal.

What you're doing is building a tolerance to fun, a boredom threshold for life. And the worst part is, you might not even notice it's happening. I used to wonder about those homeless drunks on the street. How could they possibly let themselves get that bad? How could they put alcohol ahead of literally everything in their life? This is how. Little by little, alcohol replaced everything meaningful and fun they used to enjoy.

TODAY, think back to a year or so, or maybe even farther if you've been drinking regularly for a long time. What activities did you used to enjoy? What did you like to do when you were younger? Baseball? Swimming? Skiing? Try to think about when you last engaged in that activity and had fun. Who was with you? Were you laughing? How did you feel physically? How did you feel emotionally? What was it that made you love that activity? If you haven't done it in a long time, what made you stop?

The goal here isn't necessarily for you to pick up an old hobby. I want you to notice whether your tolerance for alcohol has also rendered other activities and people less meaningful or enjoyable. Let your subconscious mind mull it over for a while. Is it worth abandoning everything you think is fun and pleasurable in life for a few fleeting moments of artificial fun? You now know what's happening in your brain chemically. It's not like you can simply decide to have more fun with alcohol in your system. Your brain *will* counteract the alcohol. It's trying to save your life. Maybe all the extra calories, hangovers, and regret just aren't worth it. You get to decide.

Day 18 Reflections from alcoholexperiment.com

"My husband came home after being away for a week, and he commented on the amount of weight I'd lost. I've been eating more than ever. I'm crediting this to not drinking! I really hadn't noticed. I've been busy. He said I looked better, too. Not that I want to define myself by what others say, but this was definitely motivation to continue."
—MIA

"My greatest passions in life are reading, creativity—writing poems and drawing, having fun adventures with my friends in the bush, and being dramatic with my friends and sisters. We always make up funny skits and have a laugh. I was on the phone with my sister last night reminiscing, and I told her that we'd had so much fun without booze when we were younger. We were just free and in the moment. If we could be that way then, we can do it now. What a profound realization."
—TERRI

❘ DAY 19 ❘

Dealing with Depression

Stars can't shine without darkness.
—ANONYMOUS

Often it feels like depression and alcohol are linked in this chicken-and-egg scenario. Which comes first? Alcohol itself is labeled as a depressant, meaning it suppresses your arousal levels and reduces excitability. It's capable of causing both sadness and depression, as well as making a sad situation worse. I've personally struggled with anxiety and depression since I was young, and I was officially diagnosed with clinical depression almost two decades ago. So, as you might imagine, I'm particularly interested in this area of research.

When you use alcohol to numb your sadness, you're also numbing anything that makes you feel happy. And that only worsens your depression. It's kind of like when you get a shot of novocaine at the dentist. You may only need work done on one tooth, but the chemical in the shot affects the whole side of your face. So on one side of the chicken-and-egg scenario, alcohol does chemically cause depression.

On the other side, depression can actually lead to an alcohol addiction. In my case, I can remember being filled with anxiety and depression from a young age. Your experience may be different, but I used to look outside myself for something I was missing that would make me happy—a boyfriend, a husband, a career, a house, a child. As I achieved these things one by one, I would still feel this sadness and emptiness. So I'd become obsessed with the next thing I was missing. Eventually, I had it all—I had a marriage and a family, I was at the top of my profession, I had a beautiful house in Colorado. I couldn't think of a single thing I needed to make me happy. Yet I was depressed. And that's when my drinking became a real problem. I was already a daily drinker, but it wasn't until I no longer had anything external to obsess over that I turned to alcohol to numb my pain. Even though I was on three different prescribed depression medications, nothing solved the problem.

In a way, I believe my alcohol addiction saved my life because it forced me to turn inward and figure out what was actually going on. It forced me to finally face my depression head-on. In that moment, I began a painful, terrifying, life-affirming journey inside to know myself and accept myself just as I am, sadness and all. And I have to confess, I felt so much guilt about being sad given my amazing external circumstances.

▌ WHAT MATTERS

Whether your depression came first, or your alcohol is causing it, doesn't matter. What matters is that the feelings are there and that you want to feel differently. And at least for me, I wanted to have a box to put those feelings into. A reason for them. Once I stopped drinking, my mind kept seeking a reason for my feelings of sadness. And the only thing that had changed was that I no longer drank. So that's what my brain latched on to. Little thoughts came into my head: *You weren't this sad when you drank. It's not fair that you've cut out such a powerful tool. Maybe just one glass of wine would make you feel better. It's the abstinence that's making you feel sad.* Of course, I knew these thoughts weren't true, especially later, when I applied the ACT Technique to them. But that didn't stop the thoughts from being there. And when we're depressed, we obsess. We blow the thoughts up and make them true inside our heads until the thoughts become a compulsion.

So I became obsessed with research. And my research proved to me definitively that self-medicating with alcohol is a terrible idea! It leads to neurochemical addiction, and it prolonged my bouts of depression because I never had to come face-to-face with my pain. I was never forced to address the real issues. When I looked back through the lens of the ACT Technique, I remembered that I was far more depressed when I was drinking than I ever was without the alcohol. My brain was trying to trick me, and I just had to remember the truth.

Finding My Truth

It took work and effort for me to unpack all these emotions and try to understand them. It took a lot of patience with myself to accept that some feelings just exist and there's no reason for them. It took a lot of acceptance to love myself, sadness and all. None of that was possible when I was self-medicating with alcohol. I was too numb to make the effort. And my life now is so much better and I have much less anxiety, fear, and depression than at any other time in my life. I'm no longer on medication, and I have the tools to handle the occasional low periods when they come along.

Depression is incredibly complex. And every person experiences it differently. One thing that I know to be true, though, is that alcohol doesn't help. It only masks the problem and makes it worse.

TODAY, realize that alcohol could be either the chicken or the egg. In fact, it could be both at the same time. Now that you've been alcohol-free for a little while, it can be tempting to buy into the idea that if you're sad or depressed, it's because you're no longer drinking. I know that was true for me. But think clearly for a bit. Apply the ACT Technique to this. Were you this sad before you started drinking heavily? Did alcohol actually make you happier? Or did it just numb the pain for a while? Now that you've removed the alcohol, are these feelings new? Or were they present before? There's no right or wrong answer. I only ask that you be honest with yourself. Shine a light in the dark places where you hide secrets from yourself. That's where you'll find the truth.

Day 19 Reflections from alcoholexperiment.com

"This has been such a great experience. I never could have imagined how life changing this has been for me. Now that the alcohol is gone, I have clarity and peace every day. Yes, there are stormy thoughts and emotions, but they have always been there. The alcohol just numbed them temporarily. Dealing with them without alcohol makes me see how manageable they are. They are just fleeting thoughts, nothing more. So good to have me in control again!"

—JORDAN

"Depression is such an important issue to talk about. My father suffered from depression, and no one ever talked about it. I feel like there was so much shame about the topic—like you are not allowed to have depression. I am finally trying to heal this part of my life and not numb out. There is no shame in depression; it can in many ways be a gift. I am learning how to breathe through it and acknowledge pain without letting it take over. Thank you to everyone who writes comments and reads. You all have been so important to me!"

—JOY

❚ DAY 20 ❚

*Our Headline Culture
and the Science of Sharing*

The problem with the internet
is that it can be difficult to confirm authenticity.
–ABRAHAM LINCOLN

Okay, obviously Abraham Lincoln didn't say that; he was long dead before the internet came into existence. But I think that little joke makes the point that it is difficult to confirm what is true online. We all like to stay informed and feel smart, yet we're all extremely busy, *so* we don't often take the time to confirm what we see or read online. We live in this headline-driven culture where we're constantly scrolling through headlines, whether it's on social media or the bottom third of a news show. We don't have a lot of time to digest and analyze the millions of pieces of information we're bombarded with each day. So we read the headlines and trust that the actual news story, article, or video is true. After all, it's the news. It has to be fact-checked, right? Wrong. In this age of the 24-7-365 news cycle, there's simply no time to check stories for accuracy. Twenty years ago, there was time between when a story broke and when it was actually reported. Even if it was only a few hours, that was enough time to corroborate stories and double-check statistics. Journalists prided themselves on accuracy and a lack of bias.

But these days the media is required to pump out new information as fast as it can, regardless of the truth. The internet is a content beast that's never satisfied. We can't feed it fast enough. And if an organization does get called out for a mistake, they can easily change it with a few clicks. They don't have to print a correction in the next day's paper or give an embarrassing on-air apology. Besides that, our culture's collective attention span is so short that even the most scandalous misrepresentations are quickly forgotten.

And let's not forget about clickbait and fake-news websites designed to look legitimate at first glance. These are driven by money and greed. The more clicks a story gets, the more money the site makes from advertisers. The writers know this, so they manufacture headlines designed to make you curious or angry so you click the link. Chances are you know good and well that the article is clickbait, but you go ahead and check it out anyway because the headline is so compelling or infuriating. Of course, it doesn't matter what the headline says, because the body of the article (which most people probably won't read) goes on to explain that the headline wasn't true—so that makes it okay in their eyes.

SOCIAL CURRENCY

So we're exposed to news stories and content that may or may not be even remotely accurate. But it doesn't matter because we don't have time to read past the headlines anyway. And then what happens? How do such blatantly false articles get shared across the internet and go viral? The science of sharing says that people share content that gives them social currency. That means we share things that we think will make us look good in other people's eyes. As we've discussed, anything that confirms our own personal biases or makes us look smart or hip or funny—that's what gets shared. Anything that makes us feel bad or uncomfortable gets ignored. Consequently, positive articles about alcohol are shared far more often than ones about its negative effects on our lives.

What does any of this have to do with drinking? It comes down to conditioning. We see all these headlines about the benefits of alcohol. They get shared over and over again because they confirm our beliefs and make us feel good about our behavior. If we're drinking more than we want to and we see a headline that says red wine contributes to heart health, great! We have a reason to feel good about our wine habit. And we'll probably share that post. But how *accurate* is that article or video? Does drinking red wine *really* help your heart? Or are there chemicals *in* red wine that *might* help? And might you get those chemicals a safer way, like from a nice green salad? Who knows? Few people will actually dig down into the article or the actual research to find out. They'll only read the headline and keep on drinking, even though there is overwhelming evidence pointing to the *negative* effects of alcohol on the heart. Remember that repetition mimics truth. So the more often we see a headline about red wine and heart health, the more likely we'll believe it and repeat it to others.

Another example is a study that came out about dementia and alcohol. At first glance, it seemed to be saying that if you were a moderate to heavy drinker, then you were more likely to live longer and have better brain function. One headline read, "Moderate to heavy drinkers are more likely to live to 85 without developing dementia."[1] Let's dissect that for a minute, shall we? First of all, if you're scanning headlines, you probably digest only the first half of the headline, meaning you'll think that heavy drinking helps you live longer—which is absolutely not true. Even if you read the entire headline, you'll still think heavy drinking is good for your cognitive health—which is ironic because there's actually a condition called alcohol-induced dementia. But most people don't know that, and they're not going to dig into the article or read the research to get to the bottom of that headline. I did that because the headline didn't jibe with what I know about alcohol's effect on our health. Not only was the article seriously flawed, but also the study itself was questionable, and the caveats at the end basically negated the entire thing. But the news cherry-picked certain pieces of information and pulled them out of context to match their bias that drinking is good for you.

Funded by the Alcohol Industry

Many of the studies on the health benefits of alcohol are actually paid for by the alcohol industry. That might seem ridiculous, but it happens all the time. The industry is getting ready to spend in the neighborhood of $100 million on a new round of research studies. One can only imagine how skewed those studies are going to be. Yet if the results show a positive health benefit in any way, news articles will be written and people will share them—netting the industry a far greater return on their investment. They need to keep people happy about their drinking, or it's all over. So any little correlation between alcohol and good health, no matter how tenuous or sketchy, helps them keep you addicted and sell more booze.

You might think that marketing and advertising don't work on you. But the facts say they do. Oddly, they work even better on your subconscious beliefs *because* you don't think the ads are having an effect. You believe you're immune to advertising, so you don't put up walls against it. You don't question the validity of the claims. And because you don't actively question things, the pro-alcohol messages seep right into your brain, where they can keep on conditioning you to consume greater and greater amounts. And all those viral videos, social media articles, memes, and funny drinking quips your friends share with you? That's *all* advertising! It's all conditioning. And we let it into our minds without hesitation.

TODAY, think about what you're letting into your mind. Do you even question the truth anymore? Does it matter that headlines are deliberately misleading you just to get a click and make a few cents? And examine your own social media sharing behavior. Do you find yourself scanning headlines and sharing them without actually reading and understanding the article? Does that bother you? What (if anything) would you like to do about it?

Day 20 Reflections from alcoholexperiment.com

"Alcohol is the new cigarette. My parents both smoked and typically had highballs after a long day. It was the sophisticated, intelligent lifestyle. Both my parents died of lung cancer. Today we know that smoking is harmful to anyone's health—it is highly addictive and very difficult to quit once you are hooked. Very few people smoke casually. Smoking is considered unwise, and people who refuse to quit or can't quit are thought of as being addicted and unable to overcome this problem, as opposed to being 'cool,' which may have been what they thought smoking was when they started.

"Years from now we may be saying the same things about alcohol. We may be recognizing that although some people can manage having a drink once a month or on a special occasion, this is by far the exception not the rule. Perhaps we will be recognizing that so many lives have been lost and/or negatively impacted by alcohol. I am beyond grateful for this program and the learning we are all receiving and applying to our lives."   —MANNY

"I feel great! I've gone from feeling very sleepy, falling asleep for naps in the day and crashing hard in the evening, to having an abundance of energy. I've crossed some threshold. I have been healing, and my newfound energy is a good sign. The tricky thing is that I've felt my craving for a drink more intensely. I think it's because I'm forgetting how horrible it makes me feel. So I remind myself of the hangovers, the self-loathing, and the wasted days. I know my cycle with it. One or two drinks here and there will spiral downward to a bottle a night. I don't want to go back there, so I'm going to continue to move forward! It's getting better all the time! The scale has started to budge. I'm wanting to get out and move after work, get exercise. I'm journaling, doing some real therapy, and dealing with past hurts. Finally! This is totally the way to go."   —SUNNY

| DAY 21 |

Hey, Good Lookin'!

Make the most of yourself, for that is all there is of you.
–RALPH WALDO EMERSON

You want to look 10 or 20 years older? Alcohol can help! Sure, when you're drunk, you don't care as much about how you look. But the effects alcohol has on your physical appearance are hard to deny, and they last way longer than the average hangover.

| ALCOHOL MAKES YOU FAT

You might be surprised to learn that alcohol is more quickly stored as fat than excess calories from sugar, carbohydrates, or protein—or even from fat itself. Alcohol has 7 calories per gram (fat, for example, has 9 calories per gram), but alcohol does not require as much time or effort for digestion; it is quickly absorbed. Not only does alcohol provide a dense source of calories—which is quickly stored as fat—but because alcohol is poison to the liver, the liver prioritizes processing alcohol over digesting other foods (and all other tasks) and stores it as fat.

Alcohol contributes to weight gain in a few other ways. First is the effect alcohol has on blood sugar. Alcohol can actually contribute to dangerously low blood sugar levels. This is important to know because low blood sugar can make us feel bad (uneasy, tired, restless, and anxious) and also because low blood sugar can be dangerous—especially to diabetics.

When it comes to weight gain, low blood sugar caused by alcohol can lead to an overconsumption of calorie-rich foods. It works like this: When your blood sugar begins to go down and you don't have alcohol in your system, your liver kicks in and turns stored carbohydrates into glucose (a form of sugar) to send into your bloodstream. But when you take a drink, your body doesn't rebalance your system in this way; instead the liver turns all its attention to purging alcohol from the system as quickly as possible. Since alcohol is poisonous to the human body, again the liver will put all other processes on hold, including balancing blood sugar, as it works to detoxify the alcohol.

This is one of the reasons you feel hungry during a bout of drinking. Since your liver is focused on detoxifying alcohol, it does not process the food you are eating or the energy you have stored in your muscles into fuel for the body. You feel hungry even if you've just eaten. This leads to the late-night snacking of high-calorie foods that you would never consider eating while sober. When I was in college, we would do a 3:00 a.m. run to Taco Bell after a night of drinking, and when I lived London, it was a midnight kebab. Even if you do a late-night food run, you probably wake up ravenous the day after having a few too many. This is because your liver is often occupied for many hours with processing the alcohol—and protecting your body. At the same time, your blood sugar levels continue to drop and hunger sets in.

If your liver is still undertaking the monumental task of ridding the body of alcohol, your blood sugar can continue to drop even when you are eating foods that are high in sugar and carbohydrates. In short, not only is alcohol itself empty calories, but the very process the body goes through to rid itself of the alcohol often leads to a massive overconsumption of calories.

Finally, when you're drinking at dinner, your inhibitions are lowered. So, of course, you order a big dessert at the end of your meal. Your normal eating routines are just not as important as drinking, eating, and socializing with your friends. Granted, all these things can happen even without alcohol in the mix. But when your inhibitions are lowered, you're more likely to throw caution to the wind and keep eating.

ALCOHOL AFFECTS YOUR SLEEP

We've already talked about how your sleep is disrupted after drinking. They don't call it "beauty sleep" for nothing. Wine always helped me go to sleep more easily. But then I'd wake up around 3:00 a.m. as my body tried to process the alcohol, and my system was out of whack from drinking. Then I'd lie awake beating myself up for overindulging and promising to be better the next day. Over time, that lack of regular, restful sleep starts to make you look pale and strung-out.

ALCOHOL MAKES YOU LOOK OLDER

Alcohol speeds up the aging process because of a premature loss of collagen and elasticity in the skin. Your face looks red and swollen because alcohol actually widens the blood vessels that bring blood to the face. This is because alcohol is what is called a vasodilator, which literally means expanding blood vessels. The real bummer about this is that over time, blood vessels get bigger and bigger. This can lead to permanent redness or blotchiness. It also leads to a loss of skin tone. All that expanding also encourages broken capillaries, or blood vessels that burst, especially around the nose and face.

Alcohol is a major source of dehydration. That doesn't only affect your internal organs. Your skin is the largest organ you have. Instead of being smooth, soft, and supple, your skin will wrinkle and become cracked and scaly. When you look in the mirror and don't recognize the face staring back, it's not your imagination. You truly do look different.

Your hair and nails are also affected. Alcohol contributes to brittle hair, split ends, and cracked nails. Speaking of hair, alcohol can actually cause you to lose your hair. This is because alcohol causes a zinc deficiency in the body, which leads to hair loss.[1]

Bloating is another big problem. When your body becomes dehydrated, it's deprived of fluid and electrolytes. Your body will counteract this by retaining the water it already has. Your gut starts to bloat. Your feet, hands, and face may also swell and become puffy. And your weight will go up.

One of the big signs that I had a big night was purple lips and teeth. I could see it the next morning, and over time my teeth became quite stained. It's not pretty. And if all that isn't enough, alcohol makes you smell bad. According to the Institute of Alcohol Studies, up to 10 percent of alcohol consumed leaves your body through your sweat, breath, and urine. That detoxification process smells horrific.

TODAY, take another selfie. Notice the difference in just three weeks from your before photo. Impressive, right? At the end of the experiment, we'll take another selfie and you will see how it keeps getting better and better. If even a few weeks without alcohol makes a visible difference you might ask yourself if alcohol is really doing you any favors.

Day 21 Reflections from alcoholexperiment.com

"I took a selfie about a month before I started the AE. I looked dead in the eyes, red, watery eyes, no hair, no makeup . . . just bloated and dead. I took one yesterday while working a booth at a flea market. I had been up since 3:00-ish a.m., and the photo still looked better than a selfie I took mid-afternoon in my drinking phase."　　　　　　　　　　　　　—MELANIE

"Day 21 on the AE—I am fat and tired and achy and unfit. I am also happy that I can say I have genuinely started to change some of that. I am proud that I have finally found a way to say, 'I don't drink'—so simple and so powerful. Now I can see the possibilities opening before me for changing how I eat, being able to start to do some sort of exercise, and feeling less like an old lady. I am actively trying to improve my situation rather than losing those thoughts in the fogginess of alcohol misuse. It's dawning on me that it is down to me to take care of this body I am in, before it is unable to take care of me—that's not anyone else's job! I do feel weary today, but I made myself go out for that walk to the shop with my husband, rather than sitting at home or going by car. Tomorrow, I have decided, will be day one using the exercise bike we have in the study—it has been waiting patiently for me to remember it is there!"   —NICOLE

"I'm amazed at how people are telling me how good I look with only three weeks AF. And I feel even better. I'm going out to dinner and events and really not even giving a drink a second thought."   —CORA

❙ DAY 22 ❙

Drinking Due to Unmet Needs

Human happiness and human satisfaction
must ultimately come from within oneself.
—DALAI LAMA

In 1943, Abraham Maslow published his now famous "hierarchy of needs" (illustrated on the next page). He was interested in human motivation and what made people behave the way they do. He proposed that people must meet their lower needs first before they will be motivated to move up to fulfill their needs at the next level. If a caveman was starving, and there was a bison on the next ridge, he'd forgo the need for safety, pick up the nearest rock or stick, and go hunt down that beast for supper. Once we have our physiological needs met (food, water, shelter, etc.), we can move up to meet our need of safety. Imagine you're in an abusive relationship. Can you see how you might meet the need for safety by getting so drunk that you black out and forget about how bad your life is?

❙ FILLING OUR OWN NEEDS

Human beings haven't changed much over the past several thousand years, but our surroundings have changed dramatically! If we drink in social situations, it may be filling the need for safety because we feel safer when we fit in with the crowd. If we're working at a soul-sucking job we hate, and we drink to deal with that stress, it could be filling a need for security. You're trading the stress of an unfulfilling job for the security of a regular paycheck and benefits. And the bottle is how you're able to cope.

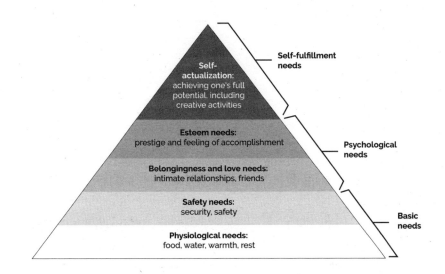

The Need for Connection

Connection and belonging are other often unmet needs. We used to live in tribal societies and extended families where human connection happened naturally. These days we're encouraged to be independent. We isolate ourselves at home and at work. We commute alone, even if we're surrounded by people on a crowded subway. We plug into our mobile devices and ignore the world, connecting with our friends virtually while our true human need for connection goes unmet. But drinking is something we can come together as a group and partake in. Social media and technology can give us a false sense of connection. But it's not the same physical, electric connection we get from being engaged in conversation with another human in the same room. We can't touch someone's arm to console them on Facebook. We can't smell someone's intoxicating perfume on Instagram. We can't taste that succulent cherry pie on Snapchat. Our senses are what make us human. A computer can take in digital information and decide how to react. We are not computers. We need that sensual input to feel alive.

We also have a human need for love and esteem, especially from ourselves. When we spend all day beating ourselves up for being stupid, weak, fat, clumsy, or whatever, it creates some pretty intense trauma. The old saying "Sticks and stones may break my bones, but words will never hurt me" is so wrong. Words do hurt, especially when they come from ourselves. So we drink to numb that pain and quiet the internal voice that's saying we're not good enough or we haven't done enough with our day. We have a need to care for ourselves, and we do that by indulging in an activity that we think will make us feel good—like drinking, shopping, gambling, or binging on chocolate.

It may seem overwhelming at first to think about the fact that you may be drinking to fulfill unmet needs. But shining a light on the possibility is a start. Becoming aware of the fact that there may be unmet needs in your life will often be enough to lead you down the path to answers. Just asking the questions below will lead you to answers.

TODAY, ask yourself . . .

"What are the possible unmet needs in my life right now?"

"How was I using alcohol to fill a need?"

"How could I fill that need in a healthier way?"

Day 22 Reflections from alcoholexperiment.com

"Very grateful to Annie Grace for sharing her story. I would feel worthless in the throes of a hangover, anxiety-ridden, and just so awful. I'm so thankful to be AF 22 days and no longer experiencing that pain. I'm really feeling confident that I can remain AF. Life is so much better without alcohol in it. I can't imagine why I'd want to go back to drinking." —ELI

"It's Sunday morning here in Perth, Australia. My kids spent the night at Nanna's house. Just 22 days ago, my husband and I would be extremely hungover today having a night off from kids. Today we're about to go for a run! After spending a night with friends watching a roller derby game, instead of hitting the after-party, we went home and watched a movie together! A movie I will actually remember because I didn't fall asleep watching it half cut! I'm having a great weekend!" —MEGAN

"Over 3 weeks! On Day 16 I said I was going to post a daily gratitude. Well, I didn't follow through with that. I've been so busy! So here are a few gratitudes to get me caught up:

Day 16: No wine-stained lips.

Day 17: Grateful for my fur-ever friends. Love my puppies!

Day 18: A husband who is supporting me on this journey.

Day 19: Grateful that I live in a beautiful place, river, mountains, blue skies!

Day 20: Wow! I haven't fallen off my bike after drinking! Grateful that I never did any serious harm to myself while drinking!

Day 21: Grateful that my body lets me run 5 miles.

Day 22: Haven't blacked out in 22 days! Love that I now go to bed, read, sleep, and get up clearheaded!" —HANNAH

||| ACT #9 |||

Alcohol and Sadness

| AWARENESS

"I drink when I'm sad. It takes the edge off."

Many people believe alcohol not only helps them have a good time with their friends but also relieves the physical feelings of sadness. They feel better while they're drinking. Let's name this belief:

"Alcohol relieves my sadness."

| CLARITY

It's pretty obvious where this belief comes from. We've all observed people in our lives and in the media feeling good with a drink in their hands. Movies and TV shows are constantly equating drinking with happiness. But we've also watched the sad drunks crying their eyes out in public after a night of heavy drinking.

I know for me, the feelings of sadness that were already present only got worse after I'd had a few drinks. So what gives? Which one is it? Does drinking make you happy or sad? Alcohol does give us a little reprieve from our feelings, but not for long. If you've ever had a drink to help you escape from sadness, you know it never lasts. To find out if alcohol makes us happy or sad, we have to understand what's going on in our bodies chemically.

Can you think of a time when this happened for you? Maybe you started out feeling great, but as the evening progressed, you ended up weepy or just bummed out. There's a physiological explanation for this. You're definitely not imagining it. This effect is related to something called the biphasic response to alcohol. We touched on it earlier when we talked about blood alcohol content (BAC). How can alcohol make us feel good for a little while and ultimately be a depressant?

Biphasic means there are two phases happening when alcohol enters the body: The BAC rises and then it falls. Depending on when you last ate, one drink can raise your BAC for between 30 and 60 minutes. My friends and I used to skip eating just so we could feel tipsy faster. Maybe you've done the same thing. But sooner or later, your BAC starts to fall, and you don't feel as happy. So what do you do? You have another drink to keep the stimulating effects going.

While that uptick is happening, you feel excited, relaxed, and maybe a bit numb because the alcohol is artificially stimulating your pleasure center. Then, inevitably, the downturn happens, and alcohol's true nature as a depressant comes into play. You become anxious, depressed, sad, or weepy. Maybe you get sleepy. Your body is compensating for the endorphins by releasing counter-chemicals. It wants you to come back down. And down you come, until you start to feel really bad.

The BAC falls slower than it rises, though, so you feel bad longer than you felt good. The negative feelings start when the BAC starts falling or gets high enough that it reaches 0.05 to 0.06. Many people don't notice the increasing negativity, though, because they sleep off the effects, and only notice the next morning when they feel terrible. And because your body starts to feel miserable at a BAC of 0.05 to 0.06, even if you could tolerate that much alcohol, you can't keep the good feelings going all night long—either because of a falling BAC or because you've reached such a high BAC that you WILL inevitably feel sad and depressed. You can't help it. It's chemical. One of the things that disguises this phenomenon is the fact that we mainly drink in the evening. Your BAC continues to rise for a few hours and then the miserable falling of your BAC occurs during your sleep. Sure, it interrupts your sleep patterns, but other than that, you are not aware of the sad feelings that the alcohol causes during the long decline in your BAC.

When I was 17, I was diagnosed with a major depressive disorder. It came and went. I took all sorts of medications and was always in some counselor's office. Sometimes I wanted to sleep all day. Other times, I couldn't sleep at all. The most serious bout I had was after my youngest son was born. It was a terrible time, and my drinking escalated because I didn't want to feel that sadness. What I didn't know then was that I was actually making things so much worse. At one point, I was taking three antidepressant medications and a sleeping pill. None of those mix with alcohol! But I was desperate for relief, so I drank anyway. Which meant I was dangerously combining pharmaceuticals with alcohol and probably rendering those medications completely ineffective.

Tragically, there's a strong link between alcohol and suicide. In fact, drinking is the most common factor with all suicides. More than one-third of victims were drinking prior to death. And statistics show that people who are dependent on alcohol are 120 times more likely to commit suicide—120 times! That's because alcohol causes depression and makes us act impulsively. It's heartbreaking, and so many people have had suicide touch their lives in one way or another. A dear friend of mine took his own life.

When you're using alcohol to self-medicate and escape pain, drinking takes on a dark side. Maybe you're trying to forget some childhood trauma, or you have postpartum depression, like I did. Whatever the reason, your pain is real. And no one is blaming you for wanting to get rid of it. But the problem is that the chemicals you're using to self-medicate are making things worse. And the more you use alcohol to try to take away the bad feelings, the more of it you need to reach the same temporary relief. And the worse you feel. The depression not only doesn't go away; it can actually escalate.

And what's so wrong with feeling sad occasionally anyway? We're conditioned to believe that we should never experience discomfort. But why is that exactly? TV commercials make it clear that we shouldn't tolerate feeling bad. Any time we have the slightest inkling of a negative feeling, we should numb it, medicate it, or run away from it.

But in reality, that is just not true. Nothing incredible has ever happened that didn't have at least a little pain, sadness, or discomfort. Consider the birth of a child, or even those awkward first dates? These things are not entirely comfortable, yet they are some of the most profoundly joyous occasions. Heck, there is an entire period in our history dedicated to the sadness of one man (and the genius that came from it)—Picasso's Blue Period.

Trying to get rid of all sadness, all discomfort, is contrary to the principles of how the universe works. Consider what a seed must do to become a tree? Two things. First, it must cease to be a seed by changing and breaking out of its shell; all very intense things. And second, it must go down, grow roots *before* it grows up and becomes a tree. Sadness is natural and normal. It is something we can learn from. When we tell ourselves it is wrong to feel sad, as I did for many years, we compound the feeling of sadness with a feeling of something being wrong with us, of guilt. It's okay to feel all our emotions— nothing is wrong with us. And imagine what we might learn or create if we allow ourselves (like Picasso did) to feel. Along with painting, so much great poetry and literature has been produced by artists exploring and being present with feelings like sadness. Feelings that we've been taught by society and advertising are somehow "bad." I have to wonder how can any feeling be "bad," especially one that produces so much beauty?

Once I figured out how to reverse my unconscious conditioning and stopped drinking, I was able to work with a naturopathic doctor on actually curing my depression. Over the course of several years, I put practices into my life like mindfulness, healthy, protein-rich meals, and regular exercise—all of which combined to make me happier than I'd ever been. And I was able to get off all three of my antidepressant and antianxiety medications. But not before I spent many times lying on the floor of my closet crying and feeling like my family would be better off without me in it. I had those thoughts. I had those times. I felt worthless.

All that seems completely foreign to me now, though. And it's terrifying to think what I might have done given the close link between alcohol and suicide. If you're in this place now, if you're self-medicating with alcohol and hoping it will make things better, consider what's actually happening in your bloodstream. Think hard about the fact that no matter how much you drink, you will come down, and the depressive effects will take hold. Depression lies to us, and alcohol makes those lies believable. So when life drags you backward with hardship and sadness, it simply means that you're getting ready to launch forward into something great! Out of the pain and sadness, you can find the courage and strength to truly heal yourself instead of masking the symptoms with alcohol's temporary lift.

Something great is waiting for you. I know it!

▌ TURNAROUND

The opposite of *"alcohol relieves my sadness"* is *"alcohol doesn't relieve my sadness"* or *"alcohol makes me sad."* Come up with as many ways as you can that the opposite is as true as or truer than the original belief.

Alcohol's Effect on Your Health

*It is not the strongest of the species that survive,
nor the most intelligent, but the one most responsive to change.*
—CHARLES DARWIN

Have you ever thought about how amazing your body is? Think about its ability to survive challenges and overcome illness. It's an unbelievably complex organism that is both hard as nails and delicate at the same time. Something as tiny as a germ can send it reeling for weeks. Yet you can abuse it for years and it will still keep you alive. We take our bodies for granted so often and don't give ourselves the love and attention we need to truly thrive. The truth is, the better we take care of our bodies, the better they will take care of us.

You probably know that drinking is bad for your health in general. But you may not be aware how harmful it truly is. Our culture tries to soothe its own guilt over drinking by finding obscure ways to say it's healthy. There may be certain chemicals in a glass of red wine that are beneficial, but the overall damage that wine can cause far outweighs the benefits. If you want to dive deep into the science behind all the ways alcohol can harm your health, you might want to check out my first book, *This Naked Mind*. For now, though, let's go through the basics. The information below was compiled from a variety of studies, but the primary source is the US Department of Health and Human Services.

| YOUR BRAIN

Alcohol slows the pace of communication between neurotransmitters, the chemical messengers that transmit messages between different parts of your brain and body. It interrupts your brain's pathways, literally reducing the speed of delivery of information between parts of your brain and body by slowing down your brain's neural highways. It slows communications from your senses, deadening them and decreasing your responsiveness.

Your cerebellum, limbic system, and cerebral cortex are most vulnerable to alcohol. Your cerebellum is responsible for motor coordination, memory, and emotional response. Your limbic system monitors your memories and emotions. And your cerebral cortex manages activity, including planning, social interaction, problem solving, and learning. It comes as no surprise that alcohol hinders motor coordination. After all, being tipsy or unable to walk a straight line is a classic indicator of alcohol use. But did you know that alcohol robs you of your natural ability to manage your emotions? This is why alcohol causes unhappiness and irritability, and why some drinkers describe their binges as either crying jags or fits of rage.

What is more terrifying is that, over time, the artificial stimulation your brain receives from drinking makes you neurologically unable to experience the pleasure you once did from everyday activities, such as seeing a friend, reading a book, or even having sex. Alcohol interferes with your ability to behave, think, and interact socially. Drinking impedes your natural capacity to remember, learn, and solve problems.

Just one bout of heavy drinking, meaning five drinks in two hours for men or four drinks in two hours for women, can cause permanent alterations in your nerve cells and reduce the size of your individual brain cells. Toxins released by your liver and passed into your brain during alcohol metabolism are responsible for poor sleep, mood imbalance, personality changes (like violence or weeping), anxiety, depression, and a shortened attention span, and they can result in coma and death.

YOUR HEART

Your heart beats over 100,000 times per day to carry 2,000 gallons of blood through your body. That's a big job. Alcohol weakens the heart muscle so that it sags and stretches, making it impossible to continue contracting effectively. When your heart can no longer contract efficiently, you are unable to transport enough oxygen to your organs and tissues, so your body is no longer nourished appropriately.

Drinking large amounts in one sitting, even on rare occasions, can affect the electrical system that regulates your heartbeat. Your heart may not beat hard enough, which can cause your blood to pool and clots to form. The opposite can also happen. Your heart can beat too fast, which doesn't allow for the chambers to fill with blood. In turn, an insufficient amount of oxygen pumps out to your body. As a result, binge-drinking raises your likelihood of having a stroke by 39 percent.

Your blood vessels are stretchy, like elastic, so that they can transport blood without putting too much pressure on your heart. Drinking alcohol releases stress hormones that constrict your blood vessels, elevate your blood pressure, and cause hypertension, in which the blood vessels lose that elasticity.

YOUR LIVER

Two million Americans suffer from alcohol-related liver disease, making it a leading cause of illness and death. Your liver stores nutrients and energy and produces enzymes that stave off disease and rid your body of dangerous substances, including alcohol. When your liver metabolizes alcohol, it creates toxins, which are actually more dangerous than the alcohol itself. Alcohol damages liver cells by causing inflammation, and it weakens your body's natural defenses. Liver inflammation disrupts your metabolism, which impacts the function of other organs.

Further, inflammation can cause liver scar tissue to build up. Simultaneously, your liver function suffers because alcohol alters the natural chemicals in the liver needed to break down and remove scar tissue.

Drinking also causes steatosis, or "fatty liver." Fat buildup on your liver makes it harder for the liver to operate. Eventually fibrosis (some scar tissue) becomes cirrhosis (much more scar tissue). Cirrhosis prevents the liver from performing critical functions, including managing infections, absorbing nutrients, and removing toxins from the blood. This can result in liver cancer and type 2 diabetes. Twenty-five percent of heavy drinkers will develop cirrhosis.

YOUR IMMUNE SYSTEM

Germs surround us, making our immune system our most important tool for fighting off disease. Our skin is the first line of defense against infection and disease. But if germs do make it into the body, we have two systems that provide defense: the innate system, which fends off first-time germ exposure, and the adaptive system, which retains information about prior germ invasions and promptly defeats repeat attackers. Alcohol suppresses both systems.

Our immune system uses small proteins called cytokines to send out chemical messages about infection in a kind of early-alert system. Alcohol disrupts the production of cytokines. When working correctly, cytokines alert our immune system to intruders, and our immune system responds with white blood cells that attack, surrounding and swallowing harmful bacteria. Alcohol impairs both functions, leaving us more susceptible to pneumonia, tuberculosis, and other diseases. Further studies link alcohol to an increased susceptibility to

HIV, not only increasing our chances of contracting HIV but also impacting how rapidly the disease develops once contracted.

| ALCOHOL AND CANCER

Occasional drinking couldn't possibly cause cancer, could it? Yes, apparently it does. In a meta-analysis of 222 studies across 92,000 light drinkers and 60,000 nondrinkers with cancer, light drinking was associated with higher risks for many types of cancers, including breast cancer. A seven-year study of 1.2 million middle-age women highlights the direct and terrifying link between drinking and cancer. According to this study, alcohol increased the chance of developing cancers of the breast, mouth, throat, rectum, liver, and esophagus.

The most frightening revelation is that the cancer risk increases no matter how little women drank. According to National Cancer Institute, the risk of breast cancer was higher across all levels of alcohol intake. According to Cancer Research UK, "There's no 'safe' limit for alcohol when it comes to cancer." It also doesn't matter what type of alcohol you drink. It's the alcohol itself that leads to the damage, regardless of whether you imbibe beer, wine, or hard liquor.

Although many of us are not aware of the relationship between alcohol and cancer, it should not come as a surprise. Again, alcohol was officially declared a carcinogen in 1988. Alcohol itself, ethanol, is a known carcinogen, and alcoholic beverages can contain at least fifteen other carcinogenic compounds, including arsenic, formaldehyde, and lead.

Alcohol causes or contributes to cancer in different ways. When your liver breaks down alcohol, it produces a toxic chemical called acetaldehyde. Acetaldehyde damages your cells, rendering them incapable of repair and making them more vulnerable to cancer. Cirrhosis also leads to cancer. Alcohol increases some hormones, including estrogen, contributing to a breast cancer risk. It also causes cancer by damaging DNA and stopping our cells from repairing this damage.

In summary, any level of alcohol consumption increases the risk of developing an alcohol-related cancer. This is a discouraging message, I know.

The good news is that even though there is no safe level of drinking when it comes to cancer, studies show that a reduction in intake—or even better, stopping altogether—lowers your cancer risk.

ALCOHOL AND DEATH

You probably already know that you can die from alcohol poisoning by drinking too much alcohol in one sitting. What you may not know is that an alcohol overdose can also occur from a continual infusion of alcohol into the bloodstream over time, resulting in death that does not correlate with a single binge. Early death from alcohol steals more than 2.4 million hours of human life per year in the United States. According to the Centers for Disease Control and Prevention, alcoholism reduces life expectancy by 10 to 12 years.

This information may lead you to ask what level of alcohol use is safe. According to the most up-to-date research (2018), there is no risk-free level of alcohol consumption. In fact, alcohol use is the leading risk factor among people 15 to 49 years old, and the seventh leading risk factor for death among all ages. The most recent, and most comprehensive, study says that "the level of consumption that minimizes health loss is zero."[1] Considering how many people drink every day, this is a sobering fact indeed.

TODAY, give your body a big thank-you! And decide whether that glass of wine or pitcher of beer is worth all the health risks you now know about. Once you learn the risks, you can't unlearn them.

Day 23 Reflections from alcoholexperiment.com

"So interesting that health was the topic of today's reading–I went to the doctor today, and my blood pressure was in the ideal range (it was 118/66). When I was drinking, my BP was borderline high or outright high and my previous doctor wanted me on blood pressure meds. I have also lost three pounds in the 25 days I've been free from alcohol." —MIRANDA

"When I was drinking, I didn't want to know the harmful effects of alcohol. I wouldn't read or listen to any reports about it. I knew it wasn't good for me–especially since I am a cancer survivor–but I wasn't ready or willing to give it up. Now I want to know all the negative effects. I want to know the truth. It reinforces my desire to remain AF." —RUSTY

"I'm still seeing drinkers as crazy people! I can't believe how much damage alcohol has caused my body and am stunned that some of it contains form-aldehyde, arsenic, and lead! How does the drinks industry get away with it? I just don't get it anymore." —GAIL

||| ACT #10 |||

Alcohol and Anger

| AWARENESS

People tell me all the time that when they give up alcohol, everyone and everything seems to get on their nerves. For no reason at all, they want to lash out at people. They're frustrated, impatient, and angry, and they don't get why that's the case. This is a real phenomenon, and I want you to understand where it comes from, so you won't use it as a reason to keep drinking. Let's name this belief:

"Drinking helps me keep my cool."

| CLARITY

It's pretty simple to understand where this belief comes from because if you've ever tried to stop drinking in the past, you know that you do get short-tempered. It happens. And we've certainly witnessed people in movies and on TV getting angry whenever the character gives up any addictive substance, such as alcohol, cigarettes, or even sugar. It's easy to conclude that if quitting alcohol makes you angry, then drinking must help with anger. We assume the alcohol must provide some sort of calming effect. Let's dig deeper into this one.

You've been without alcohol in your system for a little while now, and you might be feeling on edge or short-tempered with people around you. It's not that you're always like this and the alcohol was calming you down. It's quite the opposite. You're experiencing withdrawal symptoms as the alcohol leaves your system. You've experienced this before, though you may not have realized it. Think back on a few times when you were short with people. Maybe these were moments of extreme anger or even violence, but you definitely regret your behavior. You weren't yourself. Take a moment to remember two or three of those episodes. And notice where alcohol fit into the picture. Most likely, those bouts of anger occurred a few hours to a few days after your last drink. Is that true for you? It's because, again, the alcohol was leaving your system.

There's a well-documented link between aggression and alcohol consumption. Drinking is involved in about 75 percent of all child abuse deaths[1] and half of all violent crimes. On college campuses, 95 percent of all violent crimes and 90 percent of sexual assaults involve alcohol.[2] Why? What is it about alcohol that fuels all this anger and aggression? The biggest reason is that alcohol gives you tunnel vision. It narrows your focus so you can't or won't see extenuating circumstances. You're unable to accept any alternative points of view. Let's say you leave a sporting event and your team lost. Bummer. But you've been drinking and you're upset about it. As you're walking out of the crowded arena, someone in the opposing team's jersey bumps into you. Your perception is that he shoved you on purpose. He did it to rub it in—his team won and yours lost. Since your team lost, you lost. You're a loser! Had you been sober when that happened, you might have simply said, "Oh, sorry. It sure is crowded in here." When you're drunk, you lose your reasoning power, and you're far more likely to react with aggression. You lose the power to read social cues and behave appropriately. That simple bump could easily turn into a fistfight right there in the hallway.

Chemically, as your blood alcohol content is falling, you experience a surge in stressors and stress hormones, such as adrenaline and cortisol. Adrenaline in particular is the hormone involved in the fight-or-flight response. When you're drinking, you're far more likely to choose the fight option. Aggression just seems like the right decision. And remember, alcohol also affects the prefrontal cortex, which is responsible for helping us make good decisions. It's your brain's command center. The alcohol lulls that part of your brain to sleep, so you're less able to resist unwise behavior (like drunk-texting your ex at two in the morning).

In addition to the physical changes happening in your body and brain, there are social ramifications linking aggression and alcohol. Because so many people drink, we all understand what happens. We all know drinking makes us more aggressive and edgy. So we're more likely to forgive someone who snaps at their kid or gets into a fight when they've been drinking. We all know how a hangover feels, so we're more likely to cut our friend some slack when they're short-tempered. Because we can always "blame it on the alcohol," we're more likely to give in to our more aggressive impulses.

So why do these feelings continue after we are no longer consuming alcohol? Remember that it takes about a week for the chemicals to stop affecting your body and brain. It takes time for the toxins to completely leave your system. That withdrawal process doesn't feel good. It's only natural that you're on edge for a while. Give yourself a break. Be gentle and let the cleansing happen. It might be a good time to take a few days away by yourself so you don't have to worry about hurting the ones you love.

There's something you should know about anger itself. You may not realize it, but anger is actually a secondary emotion. It shows up to mask another emotion, usually hurt or worry. If your children are misbehaving in a restaurant and you get angry at them, you might be feeling worried about what the other patrons are thinking. Or you might be hurt that they're not listening to you. You are probably afraid that your child's misbehaving is an indication that you are somehow failing as a parent. It's an insecurity. Either way, you react with anger to cover up what you're actually feeling. Anger, unlike pain or fear, is a socially acceptable emotion. Everyone gets it, especially other parents who've been there themselves.

Once you're aware of this phenomenon, it's fascinating to catch yourself getting angry and then trying to figure out your feelings. You can use your anger as a sort of warning light to explore what you're feeling, rather than masking it with more alcohol. It takes courage, but you can step out of the moment and say, "Okay. I'm angry with the kids right now. What is it I'm afraid of? I'm scared that I'm screwing up as a parent. What if they never listen to me again? What if I can't ever get them to behave? If I were a better parent, and not focused on my work so much, they would behave better." That's a lot of negativity. It's also a lot of weight to carry as a parent. Just being aware of it, though, can help you be kinder to yourself. Emotions can be powerful, but most of the time they're not pointing to something that is truly wrong.

The temptation is to go have a drink to chill out and handle the anger. But you know that's not going to solve anything. In fact, things will get worse. So here's a great way to handle your anger without alcohol—change your physical state. Your mind and your body work together to create all emotions, especially anger. If you disrupt that pattern by changing something physically, you can break anger's hold on you. Something as simple as a cold shower or getting some exercise works wonders. Screaming into a pillow at the top of your lungs can work great. Do some push-ups or jumping jacks or play with the dog. Get active!

Another tool you can use to defuse anger is to consciously try to get even more angry. I know that sounds weird, but when I tried this, it was like a miracle. Let's say there's an anger scale from 1 to 10. First, evaluate where you are. Maybe you're annoyed and feel like you're at level 6. Your teeth are clenched. The adrenaline is surging, and your blood is pounding in your ears. Okay. Try to make yourself even more angry. Try to level-up to 9 or 10. Don't be surprised if you find yourself laughing. Because anger is a secondary emotion, it falls apart when you try to use it as a primary emotion. If you are "trying" to be angry, it doesn't actually work. The feeling just goes away.

Finally, using mindfulness as a tool can help as you try to cope with frustrating circumstances and everyday anger. You don't have to sit and meditate on a cushion for 30 minutes every day. Although if you want to, go for it! Mindfulness means becoming aware of your thoughts and feelings, consciously noticing when you're upset and thinking about what's behind that. When practiced regularly, mindfulness gives you a little bit of space in your brain from the time you're triggered and when you actually get angry. Even a fraction of a second is enough to help you get a handle on things before you react badly. In that little bit of space, you can put the other tools into action.

It's important to realize that the irritability and stress you feel as the alcohol is leaving your system is temporary. I'm not saying you'll never get angry or lose your temper ever again. But the additional edgy feeling will subside.

| TURNAROUND

The opposite of *"drinking helps me keep my cool"* is *"drinking helps me lose my cool"* or *"alcohol makes me angry and irritable."* Come up with as many ways as you can that the opposite is as true as or truer than the original belief.

❚ DAY 24 ❚

Are Addictive Personalities Real?

Change your thoughts and you change your world.
—NORMAN VINCENT PEALE

Before we talk about addictive personalities, let's agree on a definition of addiction. For simplicity, and our purpose today, we can say that addiction is nothing more than doing something on a regular basis that we don't want to do. Notice that there's a conflict or disagreement in that sentence. We're doing it. But we don't want to be doing it. There's cognitive dissonance. Because the conflict is happening inside our minds, it's understandable that we might think an addictive personality is to blame.

While it's true that some people fall into the addiction cycle quickly and others never become dependent on alcohol, it's dangerous to use this term to describe people. Why? Because it puts the blame squarely on the shoulders of the individual. It makes them solely responsible for their addictive behavior—even though it's the *substance* that's addictive. The way alcohol reacts chemically with our bodies is how we become addicted. There are a whole host of factors involved, like age, weight, environment, culture, and, yes, even personality. But the same personality traits that might contribute to an addiction can also be the way out.

| THE WAY IN IS THE WAY OUT

Take my case: I'm decisive. I have a strong will. I take commitments seriously. All those traits likely caused me to become addicted to alcohol. I was strongly committed to my decision to drink. However, once I decided to stop drinking, I was equally strong-willed and committed. The way in was also the way out. My father is the same way. He makes up his mind once and sticks with it. When he was drinking, that meant he had no cognitive dissonance around alcohol. He liked to drink, so he did. And those same traits made it easy for him to stop when the time came. Once he realized alcohol wasn't making him happy anymore, he just stopped without any problem.

Take someone who goes along with the crowd and is easily influenced by others, as another example. Environment plays a huge part in whether they become addicted to alcohol. If they hang out with heavy drinkers, chances are they'll become one, too. In that case, their best hope might be to find a new crowd to hang out with or at least one person who inspires them to enjoy activities without drinking. Same personality trait, two completely different outcomes.

The idea of an addictive personality leaves the drinker with little hope. They might feel like, "Oh well, this is the personality I was born with. Might as well make the most of being a drunk!" When in fact that person may have everything they need to overcome their addiction if they were able to take a different perspective.

As a society, we revere alcohol. We love it. And we turn a blind eye to all the harm it causes. So, by labeling a person as having an addictive personality, we're letting alcohol off the hook as the problem. It also lets us off the hook. Other people might have a problem, but we're fine. This can even lead to overconfidence with drinking and make us more reckless. How many times have you seen someone drive home from a party when they should have called a cab? Chances are that their last words as they headed out the door were "I'm fine." Let's hope they were.

TODAY, think about whether you've considered yourself to have an addictive personality. Have you blamed yourself for that downward spiral and let alcohol off the hook for its part in the equation? Write down a list of your top three positive and negative personality traits, and be honest. No one is going to see this but you. Then, for each one, think about how that trait could lead you deeper into addiction AND how it could lead you out of your drinking cycle. Don't judge yourself. Don't try to do anything with what you're writing. Just introduce a new idea and let your subconscious mind mull it over for a while.

Day 24 Reflections from alcoholexperiment.com

"Well this is hard for me. I don't like to think of my negative personality characteristics, because I don't want to own them. I am strong—like many others in this experiment; I like to do things myself. (Control issues?) I am loyal, kind, and forgiving, which has led me to forgive myself each morning and start each day fresh (only to drink again that night). It is so good for me to forgive myself, but I find myself wondering what I'll do once the 30 days are up!" —LINDSAY

"I can totally see why the traits I have can work for or against addiction, I can either spiral downward or climb upward. I say 'climb,' which implies effort in this experience, but I have really not put forth much effort except to open my mind to This Naked Mind. I feel now that my opened mind was ready and happy to receive this new info and way of thinking." —MARLEY

"It is interesting that the same personality traits that can lead to the spiral down into addiction can also be helpful in finding the way out. One thing that is sticking with me is the fact that the only thing we have any control over is ourselves—we can only change our own thoughts, behaviors, and wishes. We cannot change anyone else." —BESS

❙ DAY 25 ❙

Setbacks and the Way Forward

You never fail until you stop trying.
—ALBERT EINSTEIN

Occasionally I get messages from people who have used my book *This Naked Mind* to stop drinking and then, after a little while, have started again. Sometimes it's triggered by a traumatic event, like a death in the family. Sometimes it creeps up on them slowly. They figure they can handle themselves for one night, but then one night of drinking turns into a week and then into a month. At some point, they recognize they're no longer in control.

If you make a decision to stop drinking beyond this 30-day experiment and you end up slipping, it's important that you relax and don't beat yourself up. It doesn't mean that you're an "incurable addict" or a bad person. And it certainly doesn't mean that you're beyond hope. All it means is that you're human. People get to the end of the 30-day experiment and they're full of excitement. They feel empowered, like a light came on in their brains and they can suddenly see the truth. But we all live in the real world, and the real world is full of pro-drinking messages. Alcohol advertising is everywhere. Our friends might pressure us to drink, even though they know we don't want to. You might think you're immune to this kind of pressure, but it's relentless.

YOUR PERSPECTIVE IS FOREVER CHANGED

The beautiful thing is that by reading the daily lessons and going through the exercises, you've learned a skill. You understand cognitive dissonance and how to resolve it without resorting to numbing out. You have the tools and you know how to use them! That's such good news.

When I first started to question my drinking, it took almost a year of education and exploration before I finally resolved my dissonance for good. And for all I know, I may have to do it again in the future. At the moment, I feel like I'll never touch another drink. I just don't have a desire for it anymore. But I'm well aware that no one is immune, and the desire could come back. I doubt it will, but if it does, I know what to do.

Reframe Mistakes as Necessary Experience

I live in Colorado, and we get a lot of snow in the winter. Driving on snow takes special skill. You need to turn on your four-wheel drive. You need to slow down and allow extra time to get to your destination. But sure as anything, when the first snowfall of the season hits, people drive like idiots! Because they've forgotten what it feels like to lose control of their vehicle, even for a few seconds. Cars and trucks slide off the road, and the night sky is lit up with red and blue lights from police cars trying to rescue stranded motorists. It's like everyone gets amnesia between April and October. Once the next snowfall comes, we remember. We're more cautious. We learn from our mistakes.

Regaining control of your drinking might take a few tries. You might feel like you've got a handle on it, and then suddenly you're right back where you started. Don't blame yourself or beat yourself up. Forgive yourself and learn from the experience. Go back to your lists from Day 1 and say, "Okay, what needs to happen from here so I can regain control?"

I believe it gets easier every time you do it, because your subconscious mind has more control over your behavior than the alcohol does. Every time you go back and repeat the abstinence period, you are subconsciously reinforcing your desire to stay in control. When your subconscious and your conscious mind are in harmony, YOU are back in the driver's seat.

TODAY, remember that as long as you're alive, you'll never run out of chances to regain control of your life. The only way to fail at this is to give up and stop trying.

Day 25 Reflections from alcoholexperiment.com

"It is amazing how fast the time has gone—25 days is just amazing to me. I did have two slips, and really took stock in what my triggers are. I am so grateful to learn so much about myself, and proud that I can be in charge of my decisions. I continue to work on self-love every day, and I do have a lot of work to do. However, I truly believe the alcohol moves me right back to self-loathing. There is nothing fun about drinking for me. That didn't take long to realize. I see it more of a habitual ritual, which has to change for me to truly love myself and be my best me."   —KATHLEEN

"Going alcohol-free is the tip of the iceberg to so many other life-changing, positive ways! Freedom! I had no idea this process would start a reinvention of my life."   —LAURA

"After 25 days on the program, I couldn't be happier! Last night I went out with my wife, children, grandchildren, and in-laws for dinner. Wore my favorite pants that I haven't been able to fit into for 10 years! I looked better and felt great, and when asked what I wanted to drink, I just said I would have a Coke!

"My daughter said, 'You look great, Dad!' That made me feel even better!

"People were drinking all around me, as it was a licensed venue, but I felt very strong, almost superior, and did not for one moment feel like an alcoholic drink.

"In the past, I may have felt pressured to have a drink, but I just don't care what other people think anymore. In the past, if I didn't have a drink (or not much), I would have a drink when I got home. Last night came home, had an ice cream and herbal tea, watched some TV, went to bed, slept well, and woke up early to go to the gym. That's my new life! Thanks, Annie!"

—DARBY

❙ DAY 26 ❙

Liberation vs. Fixation

Freedom is realizing you have a choice.
—T. F. HODGE

Sometimes it's hard to tell when alcohol is actually running the show. We tend to rationalize and feel like we're drinking in moderation, when in fact we're no longer in control of our actions. So I came up with a scale called Liberation vs. Fixation to help me figure out whether I was in control. Liberation is when I can take the substance or leave it. I'm in control, and I will have a great time whether I choose to drink. Fixation is when the cravings and addiction have taken hold and I am losing my power over my own choices. Here are the clues that can help you decide where you are in terms of moderation.

One of the most painful things for us as humans is to feel power-less. Ironically, we give away our power to alcohol without even real-izing it is happening. Today's ideas will help you recognize where you are inadvertently giving up your power to booze so that you can con-sciously decide to take it back.

Liberation is being offered a beer and truly feeling like you could take it or leave it. Fixation is *waiting* to be offered a beer. It's walking into a party and wondering *when* someone will offer you a beer.

Liberation involves no internal dialogue. There's no "other voice" in your head arguing with you. Fixation is talking with yourself about whether you should have a drink, if you will feel bad in the morning—

there's a nonstop chatter about the substance. That chatter focuses your mind on the drink, making you want the substance even more.

Liberation means you can have one drink and not give it another thought. You're perfectly content. Fixation means you're thinking about your next drink, often before the one in your hand is even finished.

Liberation does not come with a jonesing for the substance after it leaves your system. Fixation often means withdrawal symptoms and cravings begin as soon as the substance begins to fade away. Someone who can handle themselves around chocolate can have just a bite. But someone addicted to chocolate has to finish the whole bar that's in front of them, and then strategizes how to get more.

Liberation puts the focus on the people and the environment. There's little or no focus on the substance. Fixation puts the focus on the drink, not the party, even if that focus is how *not* to drink.

Liberation lets you be around the substance without a problem. Fixation means you can't have it in the house without temptation.

Liberation is rational. You can decide not to drink because you have to get up early in the morning. Fixation is irrational. Even though you have that early meeting, you still want to drink.

None of these ideas are universally true for every person. They are simply guidelines to give you perspective as to where you truly are in terms of moderation. If you find yourself fixating on alcohol and having internal conversations about it, then you're probably heading down that slippery slope and might want to be extra careful.

TODAY, define what *moderation* means to you. If you're aiming to be moderate in your drinking going forward, it's important to decide exactly what that means. Does it mean two drinks a week? Or two drinks a month? Or one drink every other weekend? Keep going and determine how you want to feel as you moderate. How much of a hangover is too much? Is it okay if you have a slight headache, but not okay if you're puking the next day? If you don't define what *moderate* means, you won't have any way of knowing when you've gone too far.

In reality, you're going to want to define this as you go. Before you go to that party, decide you're going to have one drink and then stop. Before you head to that networking event, decide you're going to drink ginger ale instead of alcohol. And if you're going to drink whatever you want and not feel guilty about it, fine. But make that decision *before* you start drinking. And stick to the not-feeling-guilty part.

Day 26 Reflections from alcoholexperiment.com

"I have come to the realization that I will never be a moderate drinker and I don't want to go back to the obsession that is fixation. When I hit Day 30, no way do I even want to think about trying to moderate. It won't happen and I will be back in hell in no time. No thanks!" —HILLARY

"I love moderation. I was in that group that was prevented from changing by the thought I could never have a drink again. I am using awareness and positive self-talk now to decide for myself when I want a drink. Not just drinking out of habit and social circumstance." —PATRICIA

"I was definitely fixated on alcohol. It really occupied my thoughts for the past few years, if I'm honest about it. Learning skills in this experiment has been invaluable to me moving forward. The Alcohol Experiment has taught me how to change how I think about alcohol. I'm starting to venture out more and more, and as I do, I always visualize how the night is going to go while I'm getting ready. I throw on some good music while sipping a nonalcoholic beer and see the night play out in my mind; how I want it to play out, how it will play out. I find practicing visualization gives me a little pep in my step, a bit of confidence. It's like I've been here before and I already know the ending. I chose it. It's frickin' happening. I'm really digging feeling this good." —ETHAN

Is Alcohol Really Poisonous and Addictive?

How you think about a problem
is more important than the problem itself.
—NORMAN VINCENT PEALE

Wow! You are nearly there. I am proud of you. I hope you are proud of yourself! Today I want to conduct a bit of a review and summarize a lot of what I've said about the nature of alcohol and how your body neurologically and physiologically reacts to it.

It's interesting that our culture has completely obscured the fact that alcohol is poison to our bodies. Not only that, but it's an addictive poison. Before you decide whether you believe those two statements, please take a minute to read the facts. Take off the blinders about whatever you *feel* alcohol to be, and let's look at the actual chemical composition of this controversial liquid.

Before we discuss alcohol as an additive substance, let's talk about what addiction actually is. It's nothing more than an up-and-down cycle. You consume something (sugar, drugs, alcohol—doesn't matter) and you feel better temporarily. Then the feeling goes away. You want that feeling back, so you consume the same substance again. But this time it doesn't feel quite as good as your subconscious mind remembers, so you need a little bit more. Then the effects wear off, and you consume it again. It's literally a high-and-low cycle that keeps you coming back to whatever substance you subconsciously believe makes you feel better.

A CLOSER LOOK AT THE CYCLE

Now let's review how that happens with alcohol. Please understand, these are the chemical facts about how alcohol works in your brain and body. This isn't my opinion; it's fact.

There are four types of alcohol: methyl, propyl, butyl, and ethanol. If you consume even tiny amounts of the first three types, you'll either go blind or die. They are extremely toxic. Ethanol is the only type of alcohol humans can consume without dying. However, it's still so toxic that if you take even just a sip or two of pure ethanol, you will instantly vomit the poison out of your body. Ethanol is a general anesthetic. If you inject two or three milliliters of ethanol per kilogram of body weight, you will anesthetize the human body. That means you'll go completely unconscious. Ethanol was used as a general anesthetic in Mexico, London, and Germany in the 1929–31 era, but was abandoned because of its toxicity.[1]

When we drink, we're consuming pure ethanol in tiny amounts. A strong beer is about 6 percent alcohol by volume. Wine is generally 12 to 16 percent alcohol by volume. Even hard liquor is only 40 percent alcohol, and people usually add mixers, which dilute the percentage even more. We're masking the poisonous ethanol with a lot of other stuff that makes the drinking taste better. But the anesthetic effects remain.

Anesthetic and Depressant

In addition to being an anesthetic, alcohol is a depressant. It depresses your feelings and your nervous system. Depending on how much pure alcohol you consume, you might pass out completely or just feel nicely numb for a while. But our brains react to stimuli, and they are designed to maintain balance, or homeostasis. That means if you consume something that's an anesthetic and a depressant, it's automatically going to try to counteract those things with stimulants like cortisol and adrenaline. These stimulants leave you feeling anxious and uneasy. So you reach for that next drink to take away that uneasy feeling, and the brain fights back with even more of its own chemical stimulants. And the cycle starts.

Let's say you had a hard day at work and you just want a drink. Happy hour it is! You head to your favorite watering hole and have a drink. Within a short time, everything slows down. The alcohol's natural depressants dull your senses, and you subconsciously interpret that as relaxation. You feel better, for about 20 to 30 minutes. Then it's time for your brain to kick into action and regain balance. There are depressants in your system, so your brain releases more stimulants to bring you back up. The problem is those stimulants make you even more uneasy and anxious than you were to start with. Well, one drink was good, so two must be better, right?

You have another drink in an effort to counteract the chemicals your brain released in an effort to counteract the alcohol. Confused? So is your body! It releases more stimulating stress hormones to battle that second drink. Back and forth. Depressants. Stimulants. Depressants. Stimulants. This cycle might continue on and on until you pass out from the sheer amount of poisonous ethanol in your system. And thank goodness, because blacking out gives your body a chance to metabolize the poison and detoxify your blood as best as it can.

The Downward Cycle

Here's the interesting part, though. Every time you take another drink to counteract the stress hormones, you return to a level that's *below* where you were just 30 minutes earlier. Imagine a "feel good" scale from 1 to 10, with 10 being you feel amazing. Then imagine you head into happy hour at about a 6. It's been a hard day, but you got through it, and you know a drink will get you to a 9 or 10. After your brain counteracts that first drink, the second one might bounce you back up to only a 7 or 8. Then your brain will bring you back down. And you might try to bounce back, but this third time you make it to only a 5—lower than you started off the night.

Chemically, you're fighting a losing battle. Or maybe it's actually a winning battle because your brain will do everything in its power to keep you from actually dying.

So why don't we recognize alcohol as an addictive substance like cocaine or heroin? It's the same high-low cycle in our bodies. So what's the deal? I think it has to do with time. Drugs like heroin are metabolized quickly, especially if they are injected directly into the bloodstream. It doesn't take long for numbing and that high to take effect. And it's easier to see that the next hit needs to be more powerful than the last to get you to the same high. But alcohol is different. It enters the bloodstream more slowly. We only notice that the drink makes us feel better because that's what happens first. We don't notice the slow decline as those stimulant hormones take effect. We pay attention only to the climb, not the fall. So our subconscious minds learn that alcohol lessens the anxiety and stress. We *believe* that alcohol makes us feel better. But an addiction cycle is actually taking place because we find ourselves on this roller-coaster ride. Until you look at the entire cycle consciously, it's difficult to see what's actually happening on a chemical level.

Alcohol is addictive because you wind up *worse off* after each drink.

And you mistakenly believe that another drink will bring you back up.

It's the problem and the solution at the same time. It's the chicken and the egg.

It's a cycle. And you can break it if you choose.

What happens when you allow the cycle to continue? You build up a tolerance to the poison. Tolerance is your body's way of protecting itself any way it can. Your body is smart. It learns. And it prepares to fight the battle ahead. If you normally drink four glasses of wine a night, your body has learned that, and your brain measures out the necessary counter-chemicals for a normal night of drinking. So, if you decide you're going to have just one, your body has already unleashed the countermeasures for much more than that. Which means you don't get the same effect from one glass. You need more to get the same numbing effect. It takes four or five glasses before you even feel it. Because, guess what, your body anticipated those four glasses and gave you exactly what you needed to stay in homeostasis. It outsmarted you. And over time, you're going to need more and more alcohol to reach the same levels you used to get with just one glass. The dangerous part there, of course, is that the poison builds up. And once you get to a certain percentage of alcohol in your body, the anesthetic kicks in and you pass out. Or you die.

Detoxing from Alcohol Is Even More Toxic

Here's the kicker. In order for your body to process and get rid of the alcohol, it has to create the chemical acetaldehyde. The amount of acetaldehyde that is released into your body from just one unit of alcohol would never be allowed in any food because it would be deemed too toxic. Acetaldehyde is actually *more toxic* than the alcohol itself! So, we drink. We build tolerance. To get the same feeling of relief from everyday stress, we need to drink more. We produce higher and higher levels of acetaldehyde to process the alcohol. And we don't even realize how much poison is circulating in our bodies at any given time.

How much is too much? At what point can our bodies no longer keep up?

Think about that for a minute.

Hangovers, self-loathing, and regret are all unfortunate side effects of too much alcohol. But the chemical reality of drinking is downright *terrifying*! Once we consciously realize what we're *actually* putting into our bodies—ethanol and acetaldehyde—we can't go back to blissful ignorance. Now that you know what happens and why alcohol is addictive, you can't unknow it. By bringing this information into our conscious minds, we can finally see that the benefit we think we're getting from alcohol is actually relieving a symptom that alcohol caused to begin with.

TODAY, take a few minutes to write a thank-you note to your body. Thank it for taking such good care of you so far. Tell it you understand now. You get it. You know that alcohol is actually a poisonous chemical called ethanol. And you finally get that your body has to produce an even more poisonous substance, acetaldehyde, to process and get rid of the ethanol. Explain your current understanding of the addiction cycle to your body.

Now that you consciously understand what's happening, you get to make a conscious decision about your drinking habits.

Day 27 Reflections from alcoholexperiment.com

"My biggest lesson so far is this. Alcohol is an addictive poison . . . period. Whether I just have one drink or 10, any amount of alcohol is a poison to my body. Learning this fact has been life changing for me. I used to believe that since I was a moderate drinker, I was not harming my body by drinking a glass or two of wine daily. I now know the truth and I see alcohol for what it is–POISON!"   –MIKE

"Wow, I am amazed at how far I've come! Looking at everything I thought was a problem on Day 5 and how many of those things have been resolved, or are in the process of being resolved, is so empowering and inspiring. I'm moving on and moving forward, and if I stick at it, I will be successful. There is hope. There is always hope."   –GEORGIA

"Woke up this morning and felt so good laying there. I looked back on how miserable I used to feel when the alarm went off every day and wondered how I was going to get through the day. Now I feel well rested and ready to start my day. This program is amazing. I'm a little disappointed that it is ending soon. Off to the gym. Here's to an AF day."   —NATASHA

The Truth About Moderation

Don't bother just to be better than others.
Try to be better than yourself.
—WILLIAM FAULKNER

We're coming to the end of this experiment, and you're going to have to decide what to do next. Will you stay alcohol-free for another 30 days? Or 60 days? Or indefinitely? Or will you decide to carry on as before but become more mindful of your behavior?

Before we go any further, I want to congratulate you for making it this far! Whether you sailed through without a single drink or gave in a time or two, you are not the same person you were when you began the experiment. You have new information and you get to make new decisions. I also want to make it clear that this is your decision, and there are no wrong answers. And guess what? You get to change your mind anytime you want to. That's your right and prerogative as a human being.

That said, let's talk about moderation for a bit. I do believe moderation is possible. Either alcohol just isn't important to a person because they have not developed an emotional or physical addiction and can truly take it or leave it. Or they are willing to put in the effort to pay attention and moderate how they drink. This means constant vigilance and regular assessment. And it means being willing to make changes whenever they become necessary. I know a gentleman who drinks 17 units of alcohol every Friday night. He doesn't drink any other night of the week. And he's been doing this without fail since 2002. So, yes, it is possible.

▎ THE POWER OF DECISION

But there is incredible power in making a decision. Once you've truly made a decision about something in your whole body and mind, there is no plan B. There's no turning back. And that's a good thing because it lets you escape the "maybe" trap. Instead of running around in circles your whole life thinking, *Maybe I'll drink tonight . . . no, I shouldn't . . . but sure, I can moderate for a while . . . but, oh, things seem to be getting out of control . . . so is it time to cut back again?* Let's face it, that's exhausting. When you make a decision that you're not a drinker anymore, that's it. You're free from the hamster wheel. Alcohol no longer has a hold over you because you are of one mind. Your conscious and subconscious want the same thing. How cool is that?

The key for me was changing my perspective from "I don't get to drink" to "I could, but I don't want to." What I personally wanted for myself was for alcohol to become irrelevant in my life. A total nonissue. And that's where my own experiments led me. Because I made the decision that I no longer wanted to put that stuff in my body, moderation was no longer even a decision I had to make. Of course, it took a journey to get to that point. But once I got there, I've never looked back.

The ins and outs of moderation are complex both physically and psychologically. So before you make a decision to moderate, consider these ideas.

1. **Moderation means you're always making decisions.** What should I drink? How much is too much? Should I have this next

drink? Research shows that any decision, small or large, takes energy. Decisions make you tired, which in turn makes you grumpy and exhausted. And if you thought moderation was tough when you're in a good mood, when you're tired and cranky from the effort of moderation, it becomes next to impossible. Making one big decision with all your mind, body, and spirit liberates you from the hundreds of daily decisions around alcohol that sap your energy.

2. **Moderation doesn't make sense from a physiological perspective.** Alcohol creates a thirst for itself. We've already covered how this substance is neurochemically addictive. It artificially stimulates the pleasure centers in your brain, and you release counter-chemicals to depress that stimulation. As the alcohol leaves your system, your mood plunges further than it was before you started drinking. And you naturally want more of it to get back up to that beginning threshold of pleasure. Moderation means you're constantly going through this cycle and fighting with lower and lower levels of pleasure. The effect of one drink is to want another drink. Can you see the difficulties that moderation poses physiologically?

3. **Alcohol impairs your ability to stick with your intentions.** We know drinkers make bad decisions, right? I can remember making simple rules about my moderation, like I was going to have two glasses of wine and then stop. Yet I would inevitably wake up in the morning feeling horrible about not only breaking my commitment, but also about not being able to remember how many glasses I actually did have. I hated myself for failing at moderation. The truth is that even a single drink impairs your prefrontal cortex, which is where you make decisions. So the biological deck is stacked against moderation because just one drink can damage your decision-making power.

4. **Alcohol makes you thirsty.** It's a diuretic and dehydrates you. So that next drink becomes even more enticing, simply because your body is craving liquid. And since you're also craving more alcohol (see reason no. 2, above), it only makes sense to satisfy that thirst with more alcohol.

5. **Alcohol numbs your response to normal stimuli.** Over time, the regular production of dynorphin in your brain suppresses your ability to enjoy everyday activities. And eventually, you lose interest in anything but drinking. So if your plans for moderation are even remotely regular, drinking once a week or having one glass a night, you can fall into this trap. What starts out as a "reasonable amount" of alcohol soon becomes not enough. And you're right back on that hamster wheel of addiction. This, of course, is tolerance, and tolerance is one of the main criteria for alcohol-use disorder.

6. **Alcohol increases cravings but not pleasure.** By releasing dopamine into your system, your brain is increasing the desire for alcohol. Dopamine causes a want, a craving. Then by releasing dynorphin, your brain is decreasing the pleasure you get from that drink you want so badly. Over time, you *want* to drink more and more, but you actually *like it* less and less. So moderation leads you down this slippery slope that's all about chemicals, and not about your personal strength or willpower.

TODAY, put the idea of moderation under the microscope of the ACT Technique. With everything you now know, do you still believe moderation is a good idea? Do you believe it's even possible to enjoy moderation? And if you do decide to moderate, can you remain open to the possibility that it might turn out to be less than you hoped for?

Day 28 Reflections from alcoholexperiment.com

"For the first time, I feel like I have the tools to control my drinking, which at this point is looking more and more like quitting altogether. I just don't see the point of starting again, even in moderation—at least not for me. I can truly say that I see no benefits. I'm a little apprehensive about life AF. I plan on returning to the lessons and rereading *This Naked Mind* for support. Mainly, I'll be reminding myself of the fantastic difference between my former dynorphin-filled, low-energy self, who had lost confidence in herself, and the self of late, who has regained energy and hope and revels in each day met without a hangover or cloudy head. One who feels much more able and capable to deal with the challenges in her life." —CHERI

"I've tried moderation *so* many times and besides being exhausting, I hated being a slave to alcohol. I'm not going to sacrifice the freeing feeling I'm experiencing on Day 28 just for a buzz. I know I'd be re-addicted in no time. I'm turning 59 tomorrow and I've been drinking for 44 years! I have such a hard time believing I'm still alive. And lastly, I do not miss all the self-hatred and shame alcohol fed me." —CORBIN

"I drank an entire bottle of wine last night. Not part of an 'experiment' but just a decision to have one glass that led to four glasses. Snapped at my husband over something I don't remember. My daughter told me I had 'wine breath' and didn't want to kiss me good night. I fell asleep alone. Woke up at 4:00 a.m. sweaty and heart racing and looking for water and so disappointed in myself. So the lesson today about moderation is a good one for me. I know I can go to a restaurant and only have one glass with dinner but I can't have an open wine bottle in my home. I keep learning this same lesson. Over and over again. This is not the life I want for myself, and I have the power to change it. My kids are 10 (twins) and they are watching and learning from me. They deserve better—a better mom and a better example. My husband deserves better from me. And I deserve better from myself—need to take better care of myself, and feelings of self-loathing post-drink are soooo damaging. I am better not drinking. I know this to be true. I am the best version of myself when I am AF. My outlook is healthier and better, my mood is enhanced, I am more present, I am more hopeful. I am just more. Moderation is not for me." —VICTORIA

❙ DAY 29 ❙

Tough Love

The golden opportunity you are seeking is in yourself.
It is not in your environment. It is not in luck, or chance,
or the help of others. It is in yourself alone.
—ORISON SWETT MARDEN

As we are in the last two days of this experiment, it's time for some tough love. Please know today's lesson is written with love and compassion. At the end of the day, the key to unlocking how you handle alcohol is on the inside. You are the only one who can make the change. The choice is yours. No one else can do it for you. And you have a unique opportunity right now to take complete responsibility for your actions going forward.

We spend so much time thinking, *I would drink less if my life weren't so stressful.* Or *If my husband hadn't left me, I wouldn't be drinking so much.* Or *If my kids were nicer to me . . . Or Maybe when the kids are out of the house . . .* There's always a reason or an excuse for drinking too much. The truth is, this train runs only one way— forward. Based on your personal physiology and the addictive nature of alcohol, things are only going to get worse over time. You'll build up a tolerance and need more and more alcohol to deal with the cravings. You'll drink more and more. Look at your friends and relatives who choose to drink. Are they drinking more or less than they did five years ago? Depending on their age, they might be drinking less than they did back in the booze-soaked college days. But in general, what has been the progression during normal post-college adulthood?

Hopefully, this experiment has taught you to be mindful about your drinking habits. It has given you the power to look at behavior from a different perspective. If you go back to mindless drinking, you could be headed somewhere you don't want to go. Self-medicating with alcohol is not a long-term answer to anything. In fact, it's the opposite. It only *increases* stress, depression, and anxiety. If you've got real-world problems, drinking is only going to mask them in the short term and make things worse in the long term.

I consider myself lucky to have started looking at my drinking when I was still in control of the situation. After the first or second time I drank in the morning, I took a step back and started to make some life-altering decisions. The longer you delay making changes, the harder it will be. Your brain will become accustomed to the alcohol. Remember that dopamine is one of the feel-good chemicals your brain releases to experience satisfaction and pleasure. Alcohol destroys dopamine receptors over time, which means you'll have a harder time getting pleasure from everyday activities like playing with your kids or going to the movies with friends.

The longer you're on the train, the harder it is to get off. So ask yourself, Where are you headed? What does your future look like if you don't make a change? What's life going to be like for you a year after this experiment? How about in 5 years? Or 10? Whatever alcohol is costing you now, it's going to cost more in the future.

| REMEMBER YOUR WHY

Think back to why you started this experiment in the first place. You wanted to shift, to pivot, to make space for a better tomorrow. And you may even be searching for your true purpose in this world. How are you meant to give back? And how can you ever do that if you're not your best self? You've come so far in the past few weeks. Really, you are amazing. And you owe it to yourself to put some thought and intention into how you want to go forward from here. How do you want your life to go?

Does it make you sad or bummed out to say, *I'm never going to drink again*? That's the case for so many drinkers. They have lots of memories of drinking with their friends or having wine with their spouses, and it's sad to set an ultimatum to *never, ever* touch alcohol again. You might get to that point, and that's great. But ultimatums like *I'm never going to drink again* set you up for failure. It's like going on a diet and saying, *I'm never going to have chocolate again as long as I live.* Never is a long time! So instead of that, try setting some non-negotiables for your life. These are promises you make to yourself that allow you to make conscious decisions about your drinking. But if you cross over a certain line, then you return to a longer period of abstinence.

It's important that you don't consider this a punishment for screwing up. It's simply a line in the sand that you're drawing for yourself. It actually gives you *more* control over your own behavior than if you leave your drinking up to chance. One of my own non-negotiables was about memories. *I'm never going to get so drunk that I black out and forget things. I'm not going to sacrifice my memories of family vacations or social gatherings because I'm drinking too much.* Or *I'm never going to drink so much that I puke the next morning.* Before you return to drinking, reflect on your drinking days. At what point did you go too far? Draw your line in the sand and stick to it. If those behaviors start creeping back into your life, return to this experiment and try it for 60 days or 90 days. It doesn't matter how many times you catch yourself and return to abstinence. What matters is that you catch yourself sooner and sooner every time. And that you reflect after each episode whether it's worth it to return to drinking. It might be. But you also might start to notice that it's not fun anymore. You might decide you're tired of going around and around with the whole alcohol game. That's okay, too. You can always return to abstinence. And eventually, you might decide to stay there.

Gaining Control

It's impossible to make these kinds of decisions when you don't have full control. When you're in the grips of a craving, something primal comes over you, and a neurological need takes precedence over your conscious desire to do better. So you need to set your non-negotiable line in the sand right after a period of sobriety, like this 30-day experiment. You are in full control of your faculties, and you can make rational decisions without cravings or emotional addictions influencing you. When you make a firm decision about something, it's SO much easier! You don't have to go around and around in your brain wondering if you should stay sober for a while. You know the exact point you need to do it. Then you just do it, and get your life back on an even keel.

When people successfully complete a period of sobriety, they feel so confident and happy. They know they can handle anything that comes their way. They finally have control over their drinking habits. It breaks my heart to see these same people completely blindsided when they find themselves reverting to their same old behavior patterns. They don't see it coming. And worse, they are so cruel to themselves when it happens. Their self-esteem completely disappears. If they could physically beat themselves up, they would.

PLEASE don't let this happen to you. As long as you realize you could slide backward at any time, you will remain vigilant. Use the tools I've given you in this chapter to monitor what's happening in your life. And make the decision that you want freedom and control over alcohol MORE than you want to drink, which means that quitting forever is always a possibility if necessary. Don't beat yourself up if you find yourself backsliding. Learn from your mistakes and move forward again. If you allow it, you can get stronger every time you come back.

I also want to reframe your definition of *success*. When I worked in the corporate world, we often celebrated even a 5 percent increase in sales or a 10 percent decrease in costs. If you made a 10 percent reduction in how many calories you ate each day or a 20 percent improvement in how many times you went to the gym, that would be huge! Yet for some reason we have this idea that we're either 100 percent perfect or we're failures when it comes to alcohol. Let's look at it a different way:

- If you normally drink every night, then by making it 30 days without a drink, you've made an 8.2 percent reduction in your drinking in the last year. Congratulations! That is huge.
- If you made it through this experiment but slipped up one day, you've got a 97 percent success rate! If you slipped up five days, you are still at an 84 percent success rate—that is massive!

I love it when people start to look at their drinking in this way. By celebrating the wins, instead of the blips, we start to see real positive changes. It puts a smile on my face when I go from getting sad emails from people who can't get past Day 1 to excited emails from people who report they now have a 70 percent alcohol-free rating for the month. This reframing can change everything.

TODAY, realize that real change starts with making commitments and start defining some non-negotiables—the lines in the sand that you *will not cross*. And if you do cross the line, you have a huge warning light flashing red and saying, "WHOA! Wait a second. You're heading someplace you don't want to go!" Crossing your line in the sand is your signal to step back and take another break. Maybe you need another 30-day reset. Or maybe you need to go back and read your journal entries. What are your non-negotiables? And what will happen if you do happen to break one of them? Take some time to write these down and commit to them.

Day 29 Reflections from alcoholexperiment.com

"Feeling vibrant energy working its way into all parts of my life from being 29 days booze-free has inspired me to continue on my path of abstaining. I am working on health and fitness goals and to start drinking again would be counterproductive. I am also looking for a new job, so I am putting my energy toward things that are priorities. These positive actions will get me out of the booze grave I dug myself into. I now know that daily intention is part of my journey. I know from experience that when I do things mindlessly, they spiral out of control. I hurt the people that I love. I hurt myself and am unkind to myself. I know that old way of doing things leads to deep despair."

—PHILLIP

"Maintaining my clearheaded, energetic self is more important than alcohol. Experiencing life and situations honestly is more important than alcohol. Facing my fears AF, working through problems and roadblocks, and discovering new things in life and new things about myself are all more important than alcohol. Alcohol is just a substance than seemingly offers temporary relief at best. At worst, it has robbed me of living my best life for too long. No more—I am in control of my life now."

—MELINDA

"I have decided to remove alcohol completely from my life. Should the time come when it returns, it must never again become anything but an insignificant trifle to be picked up briefly and put back down again in its place. It will never again supplant time with friends and family, genuine connection, and joy; it will never again dominate my conscious (and subconscious) thoughts and intentions."

—BENJAMIN

"This has been so enlightening. I am so grateful to Annie and all the energy she has put into this program. It has worked for me in that my relationship with alcohol has changed. I see it for what it is. I don't know if I will give up alcohol altogether, but this is a process for me, and I know I have the tools now to deal with my non-negotiables. Thank you, Annie Grace, for your hard-won wisdom and your generosity in sharing it with the world. This is a revolution."

—SUSAN

❚ DAY 30 ❚

What's Next?

❚ FIRST, CONGRATULATIONS! YOU DID IT!

Completing this 30-day experiment is a big accomplishment, and you should be proud. No matter where you go from here, you will never lose this time of learning, self-reflection, and empowerment. And while you may not realize the enormity of your accomplishment, I promise you that powerful shifts have happened. You have embarked on a path of awareness, and you will naturally and effortlessly be more mindful of your drinking in the future. What happens next will depend on where you fall on the spectrum of drinkers. Everyone is different, and your results from this experiment may surprise you.

It's possible that you found the past 30 days difficult and still feel emotionally dependent on alcohol. If that's the case, you may want to check out the resources at thisnakedmind.com.

It's also possible that . . .

You feel amazing and want to continue alcohol-free for the next few weeks, just to see how it goes.

You feel amazing and never want to drink again.

You feel amazing and would like to return to more moderate, mindful drinking.

However you feel is perfect. Remember, this was an experiment, not a life sentence. And the whole purpose of these past 30 days was to get mindful and present around what alcohol is and how it affects the human body and mind. You've done that. Which means you succeeded.

There is often a big fear around returning to drinking after a period of abstinence, like during this experiment. People wonder whether they can really do it, or whether they will ruin all the work they've put into themselves over the weeks or months. They are afraid to trust themselves to go back to drinking. It's always possible that you could head down that slippery slope toward out-of-control drinking at some point. And my goal is to help you recognize that downward trend as soon as possible. The sooner you recognize what's happening, the sooner you can stop yourself and reverse the trend.

No matter what you're feeling right now, I want to offer you a few different ideas to give you some additional insight into where you are right now and what you might truly want. Again, these ideas have no right or wrong. There's no judgment around them. Whatever you decide is good. But you have a unique opportunity at this moment. You've completely purged alcohol from your system, and you have the chance to objectively observe what *actually* happens when you drink. If you tried these strategies at the beginning of the experiment, you'd get different results because you'd have remnants of alcohol in your system. So take this opportunity to become a reporter and actually study the facts and your behavior before making any decisions about your future.

Strategy 1: Get Drunk for Science

Before I dive into this strategy, please know that I *do not recommend you do this* unless you've decided to go back to drinking. If you are planning to take a longer break, great! That's awesome. This is not required, but I *highly* suggest you do it before you pick up your next drink mindlessly.

When we drift back into drinking, we immediately reprogram our unconscious because we often drift back into it either during a celebration or when we are stressed. In each of those situations, you deliver a strong subconscious message to your brain. If you drink for celebration, chances are that you are in a situation where it is going to be fun *anyway*, like a birthday party or that vacation you've been planning. So when you have a drink and you do have fun, you've delivered a powerful message to the subconscious that alcohol is fun.

When we slip back into drinking for stress, the same thing happens: the alcohol seems to work because alcohol will numb your brain and therefore any uncomfortable feelings you have for a limited time (20 to 30 minutes for one drink). Yet in that 20 to 30 minutes you've delivered a powerful message to your subconscious that alcohol is great to relieve stress.

I recommend that if you decide to go back to drinking, you do it mindfully with this strategy. The strategy will show you exactly how alcohol truly makes you feel, which allows you to make a mindful decision about it.

But again, do this only if and when you decide to drink again. It is not recommended if you've already decided to continue your experiment.

Now, we know that going out and drinking with friends or having a beer at a concert is fun, right? But is it the alcohol? Or is simply being with your friends and enjoying some great music the fun part? The only way you can know for sure is to separate the two, which means drinking alone. There's an exercise I've used to figure this out. Basically, you need to remove all the external sources of stimulation from your environment. Anything like TV, music, or friends will distract you from the actual feelings you're getting from the alcohol.

Here's what to do: Get drunk alone with a video camera and be mindful about how you're feeling during the whole experience. You'll want to record your thoughts and sensations around the first drink you consume. And then you'll want to continue recording your feelings as you continue to the next drink and beyond. You're basically getting drunk for science! Your own personal science. To help you decide whether you want to continue on this path.

When you have your first drink, notice how long it takes to get that tipsy feeling. Tell the video camera exactly what you're feeling. What sensations are you experiencing? Is there any anxiety? And notice how long that feeling lasts. When I did this experiment, my video went something like, "Okay, this feels interesting. I'm a little tingly. I'm not necessarily with it right now, but my brain has stopped running a million miles an hour, and that's kind of a nice feeling." Whatever you notice is fine. No one is going to watch this video but you.

Then wait at least an hour. See how it feels to come off that first drink and then objectively ask yourself if you feel better or worse an hour later. Just sit and be mindful of how you're feeling and what thoughts might be running through your head. Then you can talk to the video camera again and say something like, "Okay, that tipsy feeling is pretty much worn off now. And I'm starting to feel a little bit uneasy. I really want that next drink." The one-hour delay is important because it takes that long for your body to fully metabolize one drink, and you want to record how it feels to come off the first one. And how badly do you want to pour the next one? You might be fine, or you might be surprised how much you want it.

I drank an entire bottle of wine during my video experience, and it was one of the most enlightening things I've ever done, because I wanted to know all the stages. Record yourself in 15-minute intervals. Set a timer, turn on the camera for 5 minutes or so, and talk about how you're feeling. Talk about any conclusions you've drawn so far. Tell stories. Is this fun? Are you enjoying yourself? Are you feeling more or less stress than before you started? You could even prepare some questions that you want to answer on camera ahead of time. But talking about anything is fine because you're going to watch the video the next day and make some observations. How do you look around the eyes as the video progresses? How is your voice? How is your skin tone? How is your demeanor? Is that person in the video who you want to be? Maybe yes. Maybe no.

I did this myself after about 40 days alcohol-free. Now this is *important*—you need to be at least 30 days alcohol-free in order for this experiment to have the impact it should. Here's why—it takes at least 30 days for your body and brain to rebalance from drinking, and if you are less than 30 days AF, you may be experiencing some type of benefit as alcohol addresses any of the withdrawal symptoms (both physical and psychological) that your prior alcohol intake created. This means drinking will feel better than it would normally because of the deficit and imbalance your prior drinking caused.

If you decide to do the experiment, do it alone, do it mindfully, follow all the rules, stay safe, and be sure to film it. It was one of the most powerful things I've done in terms of truly opening my eyes about alcohol. I couldn't even watch the video for years, but I knew without a doubt that when I decoupled alcohol from both "scratching the itch" of my withdrawal symptoms and from the natural pleasures of life (friends, going out, etc.), there was no joy for me in alcohol alone. You can watch my experiment video as part of the online social challenge at alcoholexperiment.com.

Strategy 2: Non-Negotiables and Lengthening

After you watch your video the next day, you might decide that you do want to return to moderate drinking. Here's a strategy for keeping yourself objective and honest about whether you're truly in control moving forward. Go back and refresh your memory on your non-negotiables. These are your lines in the sand that you will not cross without some sort of consequence. If you haven't set yours yet, you can go back to the beginning of the experiment and refresh your memory on your big WHY. Why was it important for you to undertake this experiment? Base your non-negotiables on what's important to you.

For me, it was my memories of my children growing up. It's such a finite, precious time, and my memories were getting fuzzier and fuzzier. In fact, it breaks my heart that I can't remember my son's third birthday. Even though I wasn't blackout drunk or anything, I have memory gaps. So I set a non-negotiable that if I couldn't remember something after a night of drinking, then I had crossed a line and it was time to do something about it.

Another non-negotiable for me was drinking as self-medication. If I simply "had to have a drink" because I was stressed out for some reason, that was not okay. I was totally committed to finding other healthy ways to deal with stress and uncomfortable emotions. I couldn't keep going back to the bottle every time I had a bad day or things were tough, because I knew where that train was headed, and I did not want to be on it when it crashed. Before I started drinking, I used to run or read a book to handle negative emotions. I knew without a shadow of a doubt that alcohol was making things worse.

The "lengthening" strategy is a great tool because you never have to give up drinking forever. You simply give it up for longer and longer periods each time you cross your line in the sand. For example, if I had just come off a 30-day abstinence period and broke one of my non-negotiables, then I would immediately start a 60-day break. And the next time it happened, I'd start a 90-day break. And so on. Even if I wound up giving myself a three-year break, it's not "forever"—so my brain has an easier time accepting it.

The trick is setting up the non-negotiables and the consequences ahead of time, when you've been alcohol-free for a while. This way, you're not punishing yourself for "being bad" in the past. All you're doing is objectively setting boundaries for the future, just like any responsible person would with a potentially dangerous substance. YOU are in control of the entire situation, not the alcohol.

The end result is that you keep pushing out your time frames longer and longer whenever you cross a line in the sand. A friend of mine used this strategy and eventually lengthened her experiments to be a year without drinking. After a year she no longer saw any point to drinking again. If you ask her, she won't say she's quit alcohol forever. She simply says, "Not right now. I just don't feel like it." Alcohol has become truly small and irrelevant in her life without her ever having to make a painful decision. This is because no matter how long she lengthened her experiments, she knew she could always go back at the end of the abstinence period *if she wanted to*. After a year, she no longer wants to! How amazing is that? It's freeing to know you're in control.

Strategy 3: Understand That *Maybe* Means *Yes*

If you're coming off the experiment and you're at all concerned about backsliding, it's important to go forward mindfully. It's tempting to leave your options open. *Well, I'm done with the challenge. Maybe I'll have a drink tonight at dinner.* Or *Maybe I'll have a few margaritas while I'm on vacation. Maybe* almost always means *yes*. If you don't make a decision ahead of time, you're going to end up drinking. That might be fine, or it might not. But by not making a conscious decision, you're giving up a little bit of control, and you haven't even had a sip yet. It doesn't matter whether you decide to drink that evening—just realize that it's the decision that matters.

Before you go out with your friends . . .

Before you head to your favorite watering hole after work . . .

Before that big holiday party . . .

Make your decision. Will you be having a drink? Visualize it. Imagine how great that iced tea will taste with dinner. Or imagine yourself easily saying, "No, thanks," to that second glass of wine. Once you've made a decision, it's easier to stick to it. If it's a "maybe," then 99 percent of the time it's going to be a "yes."

What's Next?

What's next is entirely up to you. But in my experience, once you start drinking again, you can quickly regret that decision because you start to realize you're not actually in control. I've seen it hundreds of times. Someone finishes a 30-day challenge, and they think they're fine. They'll have one or two nights of moderate drinking, and then before they know it, they're right back where they started. They thought they were in control, but it's a slippery slope. It's kind of like the kids' game Chutes and Ladders, where you try to get to the end of a long, winding track. You get to skip ahead by climbing up ladders, but one long chute can put you back at the beginning. You'll be moving along nicely, thinking you're about to win the game, when—*bam*! You land on a chute that slides you back several levels. There are two options at that point. Get angry, blame yourself, flip the game board over, and go grab a drink. Or you can just laugh at yourself, realize you need to start that forward progress over again, and know in your heart that you can make up that lost ground.

No one sets out to screw up their life with alcohol. There's never a conscious intention to drink to the point of giving yourself a deadly disease. You aren't even consciously aware of when your drinking became something more than you intended or when you unknowingly gave your power over to alcohol. Circumstances line up just right and—*bam*!—your marriage is over. Or you lose your kids. Or you get fired from your job. The good news is that unlike a game of chance, you do have some control over your own behavior. And you have a choice to *learn* from your setbacks.

I made a promise to myself a long time ago to never beat myself up over slipups or mistakes. Instead, I promised to treat them as learning experiences and a chance to move forward with new resolve. You have the same opportunity. Setbacks are part of being human, whether it's with drinking or gambling or being a good parent. We all have good days and bad days. The point is to learn from the bad days so you have fewer and fewer of them in the future.

TODAY is Day 30. If you've decided to stop drinking indefinitely, great! Kudos to you. If you've decided you want to keep drinking and feel you can do so more moderately, great! Whatever decision you make is good. You can always change your mind. You are the boss. And the social challenge at alcoholexperiment.com is available if you want accountability in achieving your goals. And if you need more resources for this incredible journey you've begun, please visit me at thisnakedmind.com.

Day 30 Reflections from alcoholexperiment.com

"30 days ago I was in utter despair. I was afraid but also sick of being addicted and ready to make the changes I seriously needed. My before-and-after pictures tell a huge story. I am astonished at the changes! In this month I have also fixed up other parts of my life. I am now getting somewhere that I like and I have goals. I have my zest for life again and my creativity back. I know in my heart that I will succeed. I now believe in myself and only want to be a happy woman who loves and respects herself and others. This is what coming home feels like. Thank you, Annie, for this gift."

—BRIANNA

"If you really want something, you can achieve it. I tried so many times (thinking I wanted it badly), but I wasn't ready—I didn't want it enough. This time I did, and I'm sure that was the key to a successful 30 days, and will be the key to my future success. Sure, it's hard, but you can do it if the mind is clear on what you want! Unlike some, I can't trust myself to go back to drinking moderately, so for me this is the end of a very rough, abusive relationship. Thank you, Annie. I'm so glad I found this, so glad I participated, and so proud I have come this far."

—BECKY

"Thank you. Just thank you. Here's to mindfulness. Here's to friends and family and fun. Here's to everything in its place. Here's to being present. Here's everything I've gotten in touch with over the last 30 days. Thank you."

—SAMUEL

"Thank you a thousand times, Annie, for creating this experiment. It's the best, most educational, and compassionate alcohol program I've ever come across. Your enthusiasm has been contagious for me. I can see clearly now that alcohol is disguised poison and never, ever delivers what it promises. Thank you to everyone who did the experiment, too, for all your honesty—you definitely contributed to my being able to complete the 30 days. Wow. I'm going to do the experiment again now."   —VINCE

One Final Word

Before you close this book, I want to say how amazing I think you are. I know I've said it before, but I mean it. Simply by reading through this book with me day by day, you've done something to be proud of. I hope you take a few minutes to appreciate yourself for doing this experiment.

My good friend Alex told me recently how he became an expert marksman and target shooter, and I wanted to include the story here because it illustrates a great point. When he was young and learning how to shoot, the range instructor put him about a foot away from the target. He was so close, there was no way he could miss. It was a guaranteed success for him. Then the instructor moved the target a little farther back, and Alex shot from that distance for a while. Again, there was almost no way he could miss. Over time, the target was moved farther and farther away, but Alex kept hitting it. He became an expert quickly because he built his skill on success. His confidence grew as he hit the target over and over again, and when it moved back just a little bit, that confidence kept his hand steady.

Most people learn to get better by failing and trying to correct the mistakes. That instructor could have started Alex at a respectable beginner distance away from the target and helped him make corrections. But building on failure is so hard. Every miss is a chance to tell ourselves that we can't do it.

Now some people might say, "Well, it was easy to have success when he was only a foot from the target." And that's exactly the point. When you're a beginner at anything, including sobriety, the task is supposed to be easy. If it's too difficult, you'll give up and believe you can't do it. But when you build on a foundation of success, the next step becomes achievable. You don't expect to run a marathon without first running a mile. You don't test for a black belt before you get a yellow one. You don't learn to read before you know the alphabet. What good does it do to start a beginner on a target that's 100 feet away? They're going to miss and lose confidence. They might even give up before they've had the chance to develop the muscles and skill needed to succeed. What a shame.

I designed the Alcohol Experiment to be easy and without pressure because I wanted you to experience success. And you did. Even if you only made it one day, you succeeded! Even if you didn't make it a single day but you learned something about yourself, you succeeded!

The goal was never to get you to stop drinking, but simply to experiment and take an introspective look at your relationship with alcohol. There was no way you could fail.

How cool is that?

YOU ARE A SUCCESS!

At the end of the day, this is your journey.

My wish for you now is that you take that success and let it be a foundation for whatever you choose to do moving forward. The target for you is a decision you make about alcohol and your life, and you want to make it *easy*. If you decide to go another 30 days without drinking—if that's easy for you—great. If you decide moderation is your thing and you're going to skip that second glass of wine, just for tonight, cool. You can do it.

You're already successful, so make your next steps easy. You don't have to set yourself up for failure by deciding to quit forever, if that's going to be hard. In fact, I don't say that I've quit alcohol forever. I know if I did, my brain would rebel and I might be tempted to have a drink. I like to say that I drink as much as I want, whenever I want. And the reality is that by knowing and reminding myself of the truth about alcohol, I haven't wanted a drink in years. Take it in steps you know you can achieve. And then move the target back as your confidence grows. It's your life. You get to decide.

When most people decide to quit drinking, they think they have to make it a lifelong commitment. That means that if they *ever* have a drink *in their entire life*, they've failed. That's a lot of pressure! But if they decide, *I'm not going to drink for today*—or *this week*, or *this month*, or even *this year*—it's much easier to handle.

Your brain is amazing, and you can program it to do what you want by repeatedly succeeding. If you make the target too hard to hit, you'll consistently fail. When that happens, your brain gets the message that you're a failure. And you start to believe it! When you believe you're a failure when it comes to alcohol, that belief makes your life SO difficult. Train your brain to believe you're successful instead, and you can do anything you decide to do.

Make the smallest possible decision that you know you can succeed at. All you have to do is show up, hit the easy target, and congratulate yourself on a big win.

You have all the tools you need to succeed with this book. If you'd like more support and resources, I invite you to join me and thousands of other people from around the world at alcoholexperiment.com.

You're already a success. You got this!

With all the love in my heart,
Annie

Acknowledgments

First, thank you to my incredible Naked Mind team—you amaze me every single day.

My brilliant agent, Margaret Riley King, whose vision has given my work the ability to travel the globe.

Charles Sailor for the introductions and conversations and encouragement that helped make all this possible.

Linda Sivertsen for taking the time to listen and seeing something worth talking about.

Mom and Dad—thank you for raising me to see things differently and giving me the courage and confidence to go after the vision in my head.

To Byron Katie, whose work has helped shape my inner life and, more importantly, my inner peace.

Brené Brown, whose work encourages me to be vulnerable and brave the wilderness.

Glennon Doyle, whose truth telling I am inspired and encouraged by.

Dan Harris, whose work inspired me to explore mindfulness, which opened up an entirely different aspect to my life and my work.

Rob Bell, whose faith and ability to talk about grace keep me grounded and hopeful.

Jay Pathak, your words continuously shape the direction of my life.

Thad A. Polk, whose research in the field of the brain and addiction is of vital importance.

Julie Ann Eason, whose talent in writing has made this book what it is today.

The entire amazing team at Avery, who have worked so hard to bring this important book into the world.

Most important, to every person who is inspired to ask the question "Is alcohol really making me happy?" and who is courageous in seeking an answer.

Appendix

ACT TECHNIQUE WORKSHEET

When you complete ACT with a belief or story that is keeping you stuck or causing you pain, that belief lets go of you both logically, and far more powerfully, emotionally. This means that through this process the story or belief stops causing you pain and stress.

Complete this worksheet for any belief or story that is not helpful to you or is holding you back. It doesn't have to be specific to alcohol—it works for anything!

Step 1: Awareness
What is your belief or story? Name it and write it down.

_____

What experiences and observations led you to form this belief? Where did it come from? You may need to think back on your life and even your childhood. List a few to get a good idea of where this belief originated for you.

_____
_____
_____
_____
_____

Step 2: Clarity

Is this belief internally (inside yourself) true? When you pause and reflect on the belief, can you find areas inside you where it is not actually true?

_____

_____

_____

_____

_____

Is this externally true? What external evidence can you find that supports or discredits this belief? For this part you may want to do some quick research or observations. Look around you and find evidence for this belief.

_____

_____

_____

_____

Step 3: Turnaround

State the opposite of the initial belief—in the same words. Then find as many reasons as you can that the opposite is as true as or truer than the original belief.

_____

_____

_____

_____

Decide if the initial belief is still true for you and if holding on to this belief is serving you. Ask yourself if there are any peaceful or stress-free reasons to keep the initial belief.

Notes

Day 7: Your Experiment and Your Friends

1. **87 percent of people:** "Alcohol Facts and Statistics," National Institute on Alcohol Abuse and Alcoholism, last modified June 2017, niaaa.nih.gov/alcohol-facts-and-statistics.

2. **alcohol kills more people:** Ibid.; "Overdose Death Rates," National Institute on Drug Abuse, last modified September 2017, drugabuse.gov/related-topics/trends-statistics/overdose-death-rates.

3. **the most dangerous drug:** Dirk W. Lachenmeier and Jürgen Rehm, "Comparative Risk Assessment of Alcohol, Tobacco, Cannabis and Other Illicit Drugs Using the Margin of Exposure Approach," *Scientific Reports* 5, no. 1 (January 30, 2015): 8126, doi:10.1038/srep08126.

Day 11: The Alcohol Culture Is Shifting

1. **107 percent increase in alcohol use disorder:** "Alcohol Abuse Soars for Older Americans," David Frank, AARP Bulletin, November 16, 2017, aarp.org/health/healthy-living/info-2017/alcohol-abuse-boomers-binge-drinking.html.

Act 5: Alcohol and Happiness

1. **children of alcoholics:** "A Family History of Alcoholism," National Institute on Alcohol Abuse and Alcoholism, NIH Publication No. 03–5340, reprinted June 2012.

Day 12: Your Incredible Body and Brain

1. **this idea that alcohol is heart-healthy:** "Association Between Alcohol and Cardiovascular Disease: Mendelian Randomisation Analysis Based on Individual Participants Data," BMJ, July 10, 2014, bmj.com/content/349/bmj.g4164.

2. **wildly popular study, the Holahan study:** "Late-Life Alcohol Consumption and 20-Year Mortality," Wiley Online Library, August 24, 2010, onlinelibrary.wiley .com/doi/pdf/10.1111/j.1530-0277.2010.01286.x.

3. **CBS news:** "Heavy Drinkers Outlive Non-Drinkers: Cheers to That!" CBS News, last modified August 31, 2010, cbsnews.com/news/heavy-drinkers-outlive -non-drinkers-cheers-to-that.

4. *Time:* "Why Do Heavy Drinkers Outlive Nondrinkers," *Time*, last modified August 31, 2010, content.time.com/time/magazine/article/0,9171,2017200,00 .html.

5. *Medical News Today:* "Why Do Moderate Drinkers Live Longer Than Abstainers," *Medical News Today*, August 30, 2010, medicalnewstoday.com/articles /199398.php.

6. **more than 60 diseases and conditions:** "Harmful Use of Alcohol," World Health Organization, last modified June 2009, who.int/nmh/publications /fact_sheet_alcohol_en.pdf.

7. **alcohol has surpassed AIDS:** "Global Status Report on Alcohol and Health," World Health Organization, 2011, who.int/substance_abuse/publications /global_alcohol_report/msbgsruprofiles.pdf.

8. **no safe level of drinking:** "Alcohol Use and Burden for 195 Countries and Territories, 1990–2016: A Systematic Analysis for the Global Burden of Disease Study 2016." *The Lancet*, August 23, 2018. Doi:10.1016/s0140-6736(18)31310-2.

9. **most dangerous drug:** "Drug Harms in the UK: A Multi-Criteria Decision Analysis," *The Lancet*, November 1, 2010, thelancet.com/journals/lancet/article /PIIS0140–6736(10)61462–6/abstract.

10. **toxicological threshold (or how much it takes to kill you):** "Comparative Risk Assessment of Alcohol Tobacco Cannabis and Other Illicit Drugs Using the Margin of Exposure Approach," PubMed Central, National Library of Medicine National Institute of Health, January 30, 2015, ncbi.nlm.nih.gov/pmc /articles/PMC4311234.

Day 13: Let's Talk About Sex

1. **Drinking reduces testosterone levels:** Mary Ann Emanuele and Nicholas Emanuele, "Alcohol and the Male Reproductive System," National Institute on Alcohol Abuse and Alcoholism, accessed July 21, 2018, pubs.niaaa.nih.gov /publications/arh25–4/282–287.htm.

2. **alcohol affects libido:** Lizette Borreli, "Alcohol and Sex: What Is 'Whiskey Penis' and How Does It Affect the Male Libido?" Medical Daily, medicaldaily

.com/alcohol-and-sex-what-whiskey-penis-and-how-does-it-affect-male
-libido-357278.

Day 20: Our Headline Culture and the Science of Sharing

1. **"Moderate to heavy drinkers are more likely to live to 85 without developing dementia":** Gary Robbins, "Moderate to heavy drinkers are more likely to live to 85 without developing dementia," *San Diego Union-Tribune*, August 1, 2017, sandiegouniontribune.com/news/science/sd-20170801-story.html.

Day 21: Hey, Good Lookin'!

1. **alcohol causes a zinc deficiency in the body:** "Zinc Fact Sheet for Health Professionals," National Institutes of Health: Office of Dietary Supplements, last modified March 2, 2018, https://ods.od.nih.gov/factsheets/Zinc-HealthProfessional/.

Day 23: Alcohol's Effect on Your Health

1. **the level of consumption that minimizes health loss is zero:** "Alcohol Use and Burden for 195 Countries and Territories, 1990–2016."

ACT 10: Alcohol and Anger

1. **drinking is involved in about 75 percent of all child abuse deaths:** "The Impact of Alcohol Abuse on American Society," Alcoholics Victorious, alcoholicsvictorious.org/faq/impact.

2. **95 percent of all violent crimes and 90 percent of sexual assaults involve alcohol:** "Alcohol, Drugs and Crime," National Council on Alcoholism and Drug Dependence, Inc., last modified June 27, 2015, ncadd.org/about-addiction/alcohol-drugs-and-crime.

Day 27: Is Alcohol Really Poisonous and Addictive?

1. **Ethanol was used as a general anesthetic:** John W. Dundee, Martin Isaac, and Richard S. J. Clarke, "Use of Alcohol in Anesthesia," *Anesthesia and Analgesia* 48, no. 4 (July–August 1969): 665–69.